HIMALAYAN ART

UNESCO ART BOOKS

HIMALAYAN ART

WALL-PAINTING AND SCULPTURE IN LADAKH, LAHAUL AND SPITI, THE SIWALIK RANGES, NEPAL, SIKKIM AND BHUTAN

BY

MADANJEET SINGH

THE MACMILLAN COMPANY

PUBLISHED IN AGREEMENT WITH UNESCO

'As the dew is dried up by the morning sun,
so are mankind's sins at the sigh of Himalaya'
— The *Puranas*, scriptures of ancient India.

THE MACMILLAN COMPANY
866 Third Avenue, New York, N.Y. 10022

Himalayan Art was originally published in the United States
by the New York Graphic Society Ltd. and is reprinted by arrangement.

Library of Congress Catalog Card Number: 68-28652

First Printing 1971

Printed in Italy

ACKNOWLEDGMENTS

I am deeply indebted to the various Ministries of the Government of India, and to the Governments of His Majesty Mahendra Bir Bikram Shah Deva of Nepal, and His Majesty Jigme Dorji Wangchuk of Bhutan, for the permissions and help given during the course of my travels and studies in the Himalayan regions. I owe my gratitude also to Chogyal Palden Thondup Namgyal, and Gyalmo of Sikkim, for their active interest in my pursuits. But for the authorisations and assistance I received from the respective archeological departments of the above-mentioned Governments and their allied institutions, and also the personal recommendations to various monasteries by His Holiness, the Dalai Lama, and the co-operation of His Holiness the Karmapa, it would have been impossible to reach the Himalayan shrines, much less to record the works of art inside the temples.

I must express my grateful thanks for the advice and valuable criticism of my friends and colleagues, particularly Prof. Luciano Petech, Dr Nihar Ranjan Ray, Dr Stella Kramrisch, Dr M. S. Randhawa, Mr Douglas Barrett, Dr N. R. Banerjee, Mr D. R. Regmi, Mr Kaisher Bahadur, Dr Sherman Lee, Dr C. Sivaramamurti, Dr Mulk Raj Anand and Mr Ramesh J. Thapa. I have also greatly benefited in my work from the valuable researches into Himalayan art forms by eminent scholars, notably Prof. Giuseppe Tucci, Dr Hermann Goetz, Prof. Benjamin Rowland Jr, Mr Karl Khandalawala, Mr W. G. Archer, Dr Mario Bussagli, Dr D. L. Snellgrove and Dr P. Pal. Credit is also due to Dr S. C. Bose, Dr Satish Kumar, Dr L. S. Baral, Dr D. N. Wadia, Mr T. S. Murty, Dr S. P. Chatterjee, Mr K. A. P. Stevenson and several others who contributed learned papers to a Seminar on the Himalaya organised by the Indian School of International Studies held at New Delhi in December 1965. Thanks are also due to the untiring assistance rendered by Mrs Dhyanawati Singh, Miss Penelope Hoare and Mr H. L. Taneja, at different stages of the preparation of the text, compilation of glossaries, index, proof reading, etc. I am also grateful for the financial assistance offered to me by the United Nations Educational, Scientific and Cultural Organisation, the Ministry of Education, Government of India, and by the Indian Council for Cultural Relations, New Delhi, without which the presentation of this lavishly illustrated volume in full colour might have proved impossible.

I humbly dedicate this book to the kindly individuals in the Himalayan regions, lamas and lay devotees, farmers and shepherds, drivers of yaks and ponies, sherpa porters, guides and interpreters, district officials and especially the young army officers who, despite the hardship of their living conditions, gave me an unforgettable welcome and all possible help in order to make my mission a success.

MADANJEET SINGH

CONTENTS

PREFACE

This publication is the first of a new series in the "UNESCO Art Books" collection. The series will illustrate themes characteristic of a particular culture, region or style, regardless of national frontiers. Its essential purpose will be to relate the presentation of significant, and generally little known, works of art to the study and interpretation of cultures. In this volume, the geographical area of the Himalaya is treated as a cultural crossroad, where a variety of influences have met, combined and persisted, with a remarkable continuity, up to present times. This approach is in many respects original and even exploratory: the complexity of art forms to be considered made a full coverage of the subject almost impossible.

Mr Madanjeet Singh, who has accumulated vast experience in the study of Indian art, now extends his research in this first attempt to depict the Himalayan region as a cultural unit. Dr Luciano Petech, Professor of East Asian History and Geography, Faculty of Letters, University of Rome, kindly agreed to review the text and made many valuable suggestions. However, the points of view and the opinions expressed in this work are entirely those of the author.

UNITED NATIONS EDUCATIONAL, SCIENTIFIC AND CULTURAL ORGANIZATION, PARIS

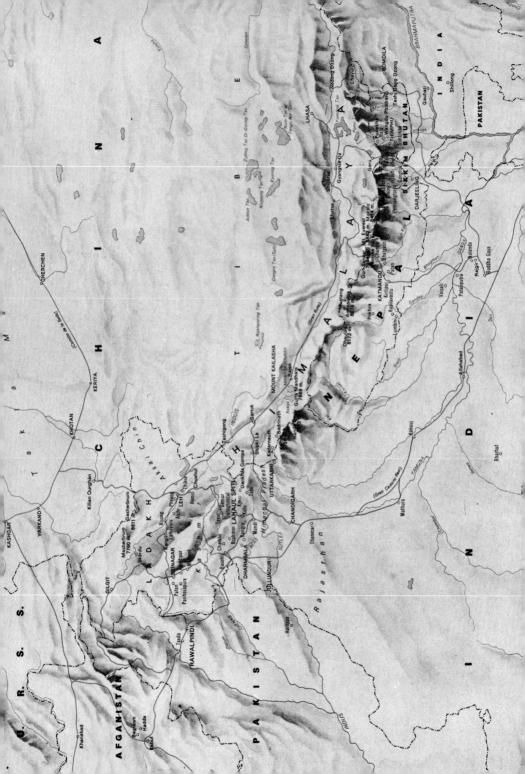

A VIEW OF THE WESTERN HIMALAYA AND LAMAYURU MONASTERY.

INTRODUCTION

The Himalaya, which means "abodes of snow", are the world's tallest mountains whose spiny ridges spread out halfway across the world's largest continent. These formidable ranges, with at least forty peaks over 7,000 meters in height, are an awe-inspiring spectacle that transcends description. The snow-covered, silvery summits spread out beyond the horizon in a landscape of gigantic glaciers and brown, barren and rugged high plateaux in sharp contrast to the green foliage of the roaring dark gorges at the lower heights, through which great rivers wind their way to the plains. These mighty barriers lie on the northern borders of the Indian subcontinent and extend in a series of more or less parallel or converging ranges from the Pamir to the borders of China, Tibet and Burma.

Topographically, the Himalaya are divided horizontally into three roughly parallel zones. Himadri, or the Great Himalaya, are the innermost rows of snow-covered mountains containing peaks like Mount Everest (8,848 meters); Kanchenjunga (8,578 meters); Nanga Parbat (8,114 meters); Nanda Devi (7,817 meters); and Namcha Barwa (7,755 meters). Himachal, or the Middle Himalaya, are the wind-swept and barren ranges leading down from the giants of the Himadri and reaching up to heights of 3,000 or 4,500 meters. Lastly the Siwalik ranges, or Outer Himalaya, with an average height of 1,000 to 1,500 meters, support alpine and temperate zones of vegetation on the slopes descending to the plains of the Indus and the Ganges.

It is in the Himachal and Siwalik ranges that most of the monasteries and temples are to be found, spreading out west to east between the great bend of the river Indus near Gilgit in Kashmir and the similar sharp turn of the river Brahmaputra in upper Assam. The two great rivers seem to hold in their arms the entire mountain region, joining hands as if in prayer in the vicinity of legendary mount Kailasha and the sacred lake Manasarovara.

Cultural influences from great civilisations have only reached the Himalaya after a considerable time lag, because of the hardships in the paths of travellers, but similarly the ultimate decline of its traditions has been delayed by geographical isolation. Even today, in the great river valleys ringed by the gigantic mountain ranges can be found traces of cultures which at places of their origin have long been superseded by the forms of later and newer civilisations. The masterpieces of ancient art preserved in the Himalayan monasteries and temples reflect great periods in the history of Asia and the world in the same way as the ruins of Pompeii give an insight into the civilisation of Rome at its height.

The art of the Himalaya is largely a religious art, which through the centuries has expressed the faith and ideals of monks, their patrons (rich merchants, kings and petty rulers and their courts) and the local people. The major religions thus commemorated are Hinduism and Buddhism. The religions and art of the Himalaya are derived from those of northern and central India and remain closely allied to them, but the isolation, the geographical hardship and the grandeur of the area have given its beliefs and the culture which expresses them a magnificence and mystery of their own. In addition, the Himalaya was open to influences from other parts of Asia, including China and Iran, and more recently from Tibet.

10

Hinduism owes its origins jointly to the people of the Indus valley culture (a sophisticated urban civilisation of the 3rd millennium BC, comparable to the famous ancient civilisations of Egypt and Mesopotamia) and to their conquerors, the semi-nomadic Indo-Aryans, who in about 2500 BC, were the first of the many immigrants into India, most of whom came through the passes in the north west. Buddhism and Jainism are reformed offshoots of Hinduism, whose pervasive influence was—and still is—felt over all Asia. The art of Hinduism, from the time of the Indus culture to the present day, has been largely devoted to the making of images of deities. Hinduism has many gods, and each of these gods has many forms, but this vast pantheon was ordered, systematised and standardised in the ancient holy text books, mostly of the Gupta period (4th to 6th Centuries AD). Each of the forms of each of the gods is assigned special shapes, special colours and special attributes to hold (a lotus, perhaps, or a conch shell, or a thunderbolt, or a begging bowl), and all holy images have to be made to exact specifications. Of course many artists departed from these precepts, but the ideals of Hindu art have remained remarkably unchanged for centuries. The three major gods—known as the Hindu trinity—are Brahma, Shiva and Vishnu, but in the art of the Himalaya Shiva and Vishnu are by far the most popular. The philosophy of Shiva, a god of creative energy, is particularly applicable in the mountains, and in his more terrible aspects he is frequently evoked as a protector deity who will save the people from their enemies and from natural disasters. Vishnu, on the other hand, appears in more peaceful and joyful forms in most of his ten incarnations. In some of these he is half-man, half-animal, but his best-loved manifestation is that of Krishna, the flute-playing country boy whose love for the cow girl, Radha, is one of the most popular themes in painting.

Buddhism, on the other hand, in its earliest and most ascetic forms (Hinayana) had no idols. The religion was founded in the 5th Century BC by a prince, Gautama, the Buddha, born in the foothills of the Himalaya. By meditation he achieved enlightenment about how to escape from the miseries of the world. After his death the charming stories of his life (in which animals often feature) were illustrataed in art but Buddha himself was represented only symbolically. He was regarded as a teacher, not a god. Gradually, however, he became deified: the Buddha image developed in the 1st Century AD and soon there evolved a pantheon of other Buddhas and Buddhas-to-be (Bodhisattvas) who were assigned symbols and characteristics and were represented in art and worshipped with passionate devotion (Bhakti). This new trend, which had a very much more popular basis than Hinayana, was called Mahayana, but it was a third school of Buddhism, Vajrayana, that became most important in the Himalaya. The practice of Vajrayana relied on magical formulae (Mantras) and magical ceremonies (Tantras) and on the introduction to the Buddhist pantheon of

THE INTERIOR OF THE PEMIANGTSE MONASTERY, SIKKIM.

goddesses (Taras). The lines of demarcation between Vajrayana and Hinduism in the Himalaya were often so faint that they shared the same philosophy and art forms and sometimes the same gods.

Broadly speaking, Himalayan art can be divided into four or five cardinal groups, each distinguished by a recurring theme of Hindu and Buddhist significance. Of these, the earliest is undoubtedly the image of the divinity associated with the phallus (Lingam), which the early Aryans (c. 2500 BC to 1500 BC) inherited from the Indus valley civilisation when they crossed the high Himalayan passes into India. Among the several lovely specimens of pottery, seals, beads and bracelets which the newcomers found in the Indus valley, there was also the "lord of the mountains" to whom the Aryans seem gradually to have transferred their allegiance along with several other feminine symbols of fertility. This significant figure of a horned deity with three faces is engraved on a small faience plaque. He is naked with phallus erect and is seated on a little throne in a Yoga posture with his heels pressed together. Surrounded by two antelopes, an elephant, a tiger, a rhinoceros and a buffalo, this figure is clearly a prototype Pashupati, "lord of beasts", an epithet of Shiva.

It can easily be imagined how the Aryans—like the present inhabitans —must have been deeply affected both mentally and psychologically by the Himalayan mountains which they crossed to enter India. Profoundly impressed by the extremes of climate and the harshness of the changes of altitude, by the heat and cold, rain, wind and storm, they invested these benign and destructive natural powers with personalities. They probably assigned to the different elements the art forms of the Indus valley, and in praise and honour of nature they composed the ancient hymns called the *Vedas* (divine knowledge). In this way emerged the Indian gods of the elements, for example, Agni (fire), Surya (the sun), Vayu (the wind) and Indra (the sky god). The Indo-Aryans also deified the Himalaya mountains: they proclaimed in the **Rig Veda** (knowledge of verses) that "these great Himalayan mountains are a most significant omen for us", and this tradition of mountain worship survives to the present day. As the Vedic hymns grew ancient and ritual developed, the deities of the *Vedas* seem to have given place to the Hindu gods, Brahma, Vishnu and Shiva. But their images, with a few superficial iconographical differences, basically continued to be in the tradition of the figure of the divine Yogi of the Himalaya, the proto-Shiva.

Another motif of the "ageless" variety seen in the Himalaya is the ever popular Mithuna, or the lovers representing the "state of being a couple". Its origins can be traced to Vac (speech) who was possibly considered by the Indus valley settlers to be the goddess through whom Prajapati, "lord of all creatures", produced the universe and who is mentioned in the *Vedas*. Later, the river Sarasvati, on whose banks the Aryans composed many hymns, was identified with Vac and, because of its life-giving fertilising powers, was regarded as Brahma's consort. Personifications such as these of the divine essence in its productive aspect and in the guise of female and male energies became another fundamental theme which has been repeated again and again in different centuries in the Himalayan arts of both Hinduism and Buddhism. In the centuries following the invasions of the Aryans, a number of kingdoms in northern and central India, both large and small, at different times influenced the development of art in the Himalaya. These include the vast Mauryan empire (322-232 BC) whose unity and power provided the atmosphere in which Buddhism could spread and develop; the Kushan empire of north west India (50 BC-210 AD) under whose patronage the Buddha image was first made; and the Gupta empire (320-530 AD), equal in strength and size to that of the Mauryas, and commonly known as the "golden age" of Hindu and Buddhist art and literature. The "later Gupta Kingdoms" (530-770 AD), the medieval kingdoms of the Pala dynasty (770-942 AD) in north east India and the Pratiharas (833-942 AD) in central north India contrived to develop flourishing and influential schools of art.

Our knowledge of the Aryans is derived largely from their great literature alone and, unfortunately, we do not have examples of the art forms of the period between the disappearance of the Indus valley civilisation (which has left us archaeological remains but no literature) and the Mauryan empire of Ashoka (273-232 BC). However, it is evident from the maturity of the sculptures of Ashoka's time that the popularity of the Indus valley symbolism survived. Among the lovely works of art produced under Ashoka is the motif which came to represent the Himalaya as a world pillar supporting the Wheel of Law. Ashoka erected numerous inscribed pillars in his extensive empire to spread the message of the Buddha. The "resplendent pillar of the heavenly vault" has a capital representing a lotus jar which is protected by the lions of the four quarters and by the deities who won the Amrita (nectar of immortality) in conflict with the powers of evil. In particular, it represents mount Kailasha near the sacred lake Manasarovara, which both Hindu cosmography and Buddhist pilgrim lore regard as the holiest of all places of pilgrimage in the Himalaya. Manasarovara, "the most excellent lake of the mind", is thought to be the divine receptacle of the universal mind force (Manas), which is epitomised in art as the lotus jar containing Amrita. The lake, which is fed by mount Kailasha's snows, is the legendary source of our world symbols of fertility.

This symbol of the Himalaya is depicted in almost every important Hindu and Buddhist shrine in the Himalayan regions. It apparently originated from the Stupas, or relic shrines, which are the most important monuments of Buddhist art. Stupas in their simplest form were hemispherical structures, sometimes crowned by stone "umbrellas" and surrounded by balustrades, which were originaly funeral mounds containing relics of the Buddha. They were soon lavishly decorated with sculptures and

SARASVATI, RUMTEK MONASTERY, SIKKIM. 16th CENTURY AD.

THE BUDDHA, WANGDU PHODRANG MONASTERY, BHUTAN. 16th CENTURY AD.

bas-reliefs, the best examples of which in India are at Bharhut, Sanchi and Amaravati. The magic-mystic meaning of the Buddhist funeral mound later came to have even greater spiritual significance, so that the Stupa was identified with the mythical mountain Meru below which was the holy mountain, Kailasha. The central reliquary became the world axis, the hemisphere of the Stupa represented the vault of the firmament and a small enclosure on the top was interpreted as the abode of the gods ruling over the earth. The apex of this symbolic mountain was provided with seven superimposed "umbrellas" indicating the succession of higher heavens merging one into another in the transcendental absolute. These theories, for which precise specifications were necessary, came to have meaning in Hinduism as well as Buddhism. Similarly, the image of each god had to conform to an exact scheme. It was built on a skeleton of two intersecting lines at right angles, reproducing as it were a Mandala in the shape of a square or a circle, within which the deity's figure was theoretically confined. As with the Vedic altar which was built according to inviolable and accurate geometrical rules, the basic unit of measurement was the Angula or finger of the artist or the donor, and twelve Angulas approximately constituted a Tala. With the help of these standard units the artist outlined the image within the square formed by the two intersecting lines so that the triangles formed by the transverse lines determined the proportions of different parts. The symbolism of the Stupa and the world pillar supporting the Wheel of Law suggested to builders and craftsmen the glorious Himalayan vision which was subsequently developed in both Hindu and Buddhist temple architecture and sculpture. The fame of Vishavakarma, the mythical divine architect of the Hindus, who "builds the heavenly temples of snows", and his Buddhist counterpart the great architect Manjushri, who "constructs the mansions of the world", spread far and wide, and their designs were adopted by artists and craftsmen in China, Japan and Korea to the north, and Thailand and Cambodia to the south east. These influences spread as far as Java, where they are reflected in the monument at Barobodur, which was named Kailasha. Similarly, the construction of the famous monasteries in the Indian Gangetic plains which contributed so much to Himalayan art and architecture were inspired by the Himalaya. "With a view to seeing Kailasha mountain surpassed, Baladitya erected a great and extraordinary temple of the illustrious son of Suddhodana (Gautama, the Buddha) here at Nalanda", states an inscription. Hsuan Tsang, the great Chinese pilgrim who crossed the Himalaya into India and visited the famous Nalanda monastery in the first half of the seventh century, confirmed that "the richly adorned towers and fairy-like turrets like the pointed hill tops are congregated together. The observatory seems to be lost in the mist and the upper rooms tower above the sky".

Both Hinduism and Buddhism have a strong monastic emphasis and it was inevitable that these institutions, which by tradition were set

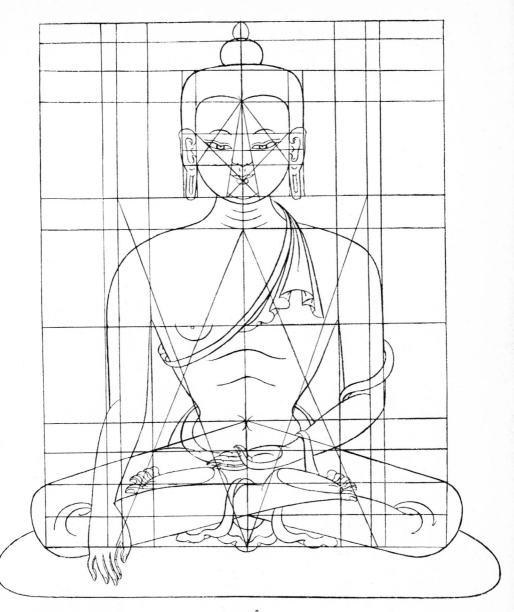

CANONICAL PROPORTIONS OF THE BUDDHA IMAGES.

A VIEW OF THE PUNAKHA MONASTERY AND THE VALLEY, BHUTAN.

19

up in isolated areas but on major trade routes, should become the basis of religious life in the Himalaya and also the centres of art, education and culture. The monasteries and temples containing incredibly beautiful works of art are invariably situated along the intersections of the enormous high valleys which are formed by the two great rivers, the Indus and the Brahmaputra, flanking in the west and in the east the valleys of rivers such as the Sutlej, Ganges, Jamuna, Kali, Bhagmati and Tista which flow across the mountains roughly from north to south. The transverse georges cut by these rivers are sometimes 3,000 to 5,000 meters deep and along these precipitous slopes are marked the tracks along which caravans of pilgrims and traders still wind their way to reach the monasteries and temples in the innermost recesses of the mountains. Also in these gaps are the high passes, only a few of which are below 4,500 meters.

In addition to the determining influence of topography, the setting up of the Himalayan monasteries follows the tradition established in western India and elsewhere. The Samgha, or Buddhist congregation, emerging from a milieu formed by the wandering almsmen of ancient India, became in time institutionalised in the shape of monasteries. For economic reasons as well as those of worship, these Viharas were built within easy reach of the confluences of water and trade routes for the benefit of the lay devotees, who were mostly traders and merchants who made donations to the monasteries during halts on their tedious and perilous journeys. Thus, by the very nature of their function, the monasteries were largely self-supporting and based on a popular culture and the broad-based community life of the local people.

Also significant in the development of the Himalayan artistic tradition were the two parallel highways, the "grand route" in the north of the Himalaya and the "great royal highway" to the south of it. The well-known old caravan route, called the "grand route", started from Srinagar, led over the Zoji pass to Leh in Ladakh and then to the area of the sacred lakes, the Brahmaputra valley Shigatse and Lhasa. From the Tibetan capital several routes branched off to Peking and other Chinese cities. The "great royal highway", in the south of the Himalaya, was the most convenient route in the Indus-Ganges plains, from which a series of side routes linked the footpaths winding along the Himalayan river valleys. It was first mentioned by Megasthenes in the early 4th Century BC, when he was the ambassador of the Greek king Seleucus, accredited to the court of the Indian emperor Chandragupta Maura. Travelling by this route, he records that the first stage was from the frontier of the Mauryan empire in north-western India (now Afghanistan and west Pakistan) to the provincial capital of Taxila. From this important centre of arts, the highway, crossing the five rivers of the Punjab, reached the river Jamuna and arrived at the great cultural centres of Kanauj and then Prayag. Finally the route led to Pataliputra, the magnificent capital of the empire.

As the message of Buddhism fanned out towards the north to become the religion of all Asia, these were the channels used also for the propagation of its art forms. Important developments in Buddhist art occurred under the patronage of the Kushans in the beginning of the Christian era. Flourishing art studios in the Kushan dominions were based at Mathura, the "city of gods", on the river Jamuna, and other centres extended along the "great royal highway" through the mountain region known as Gandhara (now in Pakistan and Afghanistan). The indigenous school of Mathura drew its resources and inspiration from established Indian traditions and early Buddhist art, while around the town of Taxila there developed the so-called Gandharan style which was created by the local talents of frontier people in touch with Indian achievements and at the same time exposed to influences from the western world and in particular to Romano-Hellenistic achievements. With the expansion of Buddhism, both Gandhara and Mathura models of its art were carried to far off sites, such as Miran, Khotan and Tumschuq in Central Asia, and the regions of the western Himalaya which were under Kushan suzerainty were also included. Even after the end of the Kushan authority, Indian prototypes continued to be carried through the Himalayan trade routes, as is evident from the examples of wall-paintings in the Thousand Buddha caves in Tun-huang (consecrated in 366 AD) and the sculptures in the famous cave sanctuaries of Bamiyan in Afghanistan. These art styles, like the proto-Shiva of the Indus valley and the Buddhist art of the pre-Christian era, are the formidable foundations on which Himalayan art was built. But, apart from stray Gandhara pieces found in Kashmir, the earliest existing Himalayan art forms actually belong to the age of the Guptas (320-530 AD) and their later period (530-770 AD).

Gupta art is well known as the high point of cultural achievement in the Indian subcontinent when painting, sculpture and architecture attained a great purity of form. This aesthetic development was paralleled in the intellectual field, culminating in an enhanced version of Vedic scriptures known as the *Vedanta*, and also the treatises of Mahayanist Buddhist philosophy which were to form the basis of the development of Buddhism in the Himalaya. During this period Buddhism had already been transformed from the Hinayana to the Mahayana doctrine, and the Buddhist treatises of early centuries such as the *Saddharma Pundarika* and the *Mahavastu* shew that the Buddha was no longer regarded as a mortal teacher but as superhuman, eternal and supreme.

The influence of the great Buddhist monasteries in the Indian Gangetic plains rapidly increased because they not only served as theological colleges but also contained scriptoria for the illustration and copying of manuscripts and workshops for the casting of bronze images. Here also were stored the art textbooks of the Gupta period, containing rules of construction and composition, such as the *Vishnudharmottaram*, the

SATI, TALEJU BHAVANI TEMPLE, BHATGAON. 15th CENTURY AD.

SKETCH DEPICTING A SCENE FROM THE WHEEL OF EXISTENCE,
THIKSE MONASTERY, LADAKH. 15th—16th CENTURY AD.

Bharata Natya Shastra and the *Manasara*, as well as the treatises of
the later Gupta period, the *Vastu Shastra* for architecture and the
Shilpa Shastra for sculpture and painting. From all over the Buddhist
world, pilgrims and pupils came to study at these "universities" and
took back to their native lands portable examples of art forms which
increased their understanding of both the instructions of the earlier
Mahayana teachers and the precepts of the later writers of Tantric
texts. Even noted foreign envoys, such as the Chinese Wang Hsuan-tse,

VASUDHARA, ALCHI MONASTERY, LADAKH. 11th—12th CENTURY AD.

SKETCH DEPICTING A SCENE FROM THE WHEEL OF EXISTENCE,
THIKSE MONASTERY, LADAKH. 15th—16th CENTURY AD.

brought back from these monasteries in India religious texts and
contingents of artists and scholars. Similarly, great Indian missionaries,
whose footsteps are still worshipped in several monasteries in the
Himalaya, were also instrumental in spreading art styles developed in
the major monasteries, the Mahaviharas. Among the eminent teachers
who crossed the Himalaya on such missions, and were themselves
deified, were Padmasambhava and Atisha in the Himalaya and Tibet,
Amoghavajra in China, and Dhyana Bhadra in Korea.

27

SCENES FROM THE BUDDHA'S LIFE, ALCHI MONASTERY, LADAKH.
15th CENTURY AD.

The Guptas, under whose patronage Buddhist art continued to flourish, themselves mostly venerated Vishnu. At first he was depicted with his consort Lakshmi, either sitting on his vehicle, the sun-eagle Garuda, or sleeping on the serpent Ananta. But in the face of the 5th Century AD, the Gupta pantheon incorporated new "protector" gods, such as the semi-animal forms of Vishnu, the Varaha (boar) and Narasimha (man-lion). Help was also sought from Shiva, the lord of the mountains who had been almost forgotten by the Guptas during their ascendency. Shiva now appeared in his more demoniac aspect. He became Bhairava "the terrible destroyer", indulging in revelry and furious Tandava dances, while his awe-inspiring consort Devi, as Durga Mahishamardini, "the slayer of the bull demon", is no longer Parvati, the peaceful, fair daughter of the Himalaya. Their sons, six-headed Karttikeya and the elephant-headed Ganesha, also made their appearance.

The man-animal configuration added a third motif to the most important recurring anthropomorphic themes in both Hindu and Buddhist art which were particularly popular in the Himalaya, the other two being the divine Yogi of the Himalaya and the Mithuna. It is advisable to keep in mind these fundamental and "timeless" landmarks in art to avoid being lost in the baffling variety of deities that subsequently appeared on the Himalayan scene. The later gods and goddesses were essentially different manifestations, permutations and combinations of these basic art forms. An ensemble of these fundamental motifs and several other subsidiary symbols which became very popular in the Himalaya is the Wheel of Existence. First seen in Gupta period painting at the Ajanta caves in India, it sums up both pictorially and philosophically the Hindu and Buddhist view of life and of the causes of human sorrow.

Such ideas predominate in the art style of the later Gupta period, which penetrated into the Siwalik ranges, Kashmir and Nepal, and then laid the foundation of religious art in Tibet. The beginning of the T'ang dynasty in China in the 7th Century AD similarly opened a new era of predominantly Gupta influence in Central Asia. At this time China had become a great united power and established close cultural relations with India. The western branch of Gupta art in Kashmir formed the main nucleus around which was built the art style of the Karkota dynasty, which was at its height under the famous ruler Lalitaditya (c. 725-756). Kashmir, intimately connected with India since the time of Ashoka, preserved in the isolation of its mountains the ideals of both Gandhara and Gupta art, as is revealed by a number of stucco and terracotta sculptures from the Ushkar monastery. At the same period, further east in the Punjab Hills, a marvellous renaissance in art—especially in bronze—was ushered in by the outstanding ruler Meruvarman. The same art forms were also responsible for the mixed Pratihara-Kashmiri art of the kind which subsequently developed in the Siwalik ranges. The varied influences which surrounded the north-

MERCHANTS ON PONIES ARRIVING AT A FESTIVAL.

western Himalaya naturally introduced some new elements of style, thus modifying the Kashmiri style to some extent. These included Sassanian, Khotanese and Uighur influences, the Chinese ideals of the Six Dynasty period and later T'ang mannerism. After Lalitaditya the Kashmiri style continued to flourish first under Avantivarman and Shankaravarman, then under queen Didda and her successors, Ananta-deva and Kalasha. This style then penetrated towards the eastern Himalaya and, travelling by the "grand route", was mainly responsible for the lovely wall-paintings and wooden sculptures still seen in the beautiful monastery of Alchi in Ladakh, in the Tabo monastery in the Spiti valley and also in several shrines in western Tibet, such as the "Red Temple" at Tsaparang.

During the 7th Century, Nepal, too, witnessed an exciting period in its art history under king Amshuvarman (593-621 AD), who was a contem-porary of two great monarchs, Harshavardhana in India and Srongtsen-

gampo in Tibet. Tradition has it that Amshuvarman's daughter, who married Srongtsen-gampo, was among the first to introduce Buddhist art in Tibet through a sandalwood image of the Buddha which she carried to Lhasa as a wedding present. However, unlike the stylistic progress of art in the western Himalaya where Gupta mannerism merged with peripheral influences from other civilisations to produce the Kashmiri style, the Gupta style in Nepal continued unchallenged until about the end of the 8th Century AD. But a great renaissance of Buddhism and Buddhist art began in the 9th Century, when Vajrayana Buddhism brought Nepal into intimate contact with the Pala culture of Bengal and Bihar. So strong was its effect that practically every building in the Kathmandu valley became a temple and a store house of its products. From this period onwards, the Pala school of art, more than any other style, exercised immense influence in moulding the art of the Himalaya. Models carved out of bluish-black stone, and paintings which can still be seen in a few surviving palm leaf manuscripts depicting deities of the Buddhist pantheon, had an overwhelming influence on Himalayan art forms. These traditions penetrated into Tibet not only by way of Nepal but also via Ladakh and the Punjab Hills.

This culture flourished at the great monastic establishments at Bodh Gaya, Nalanda, Odantapuri and Vikramashila, which were then dominated by Tantricism in which reliance on ritual and a mixture of mysticism, religious dogma, psychic exercises, magic and superstition marked the gradual absorption of Buddhism into Tantric Hinduism. The Tantric cult which is associated with the Shakti or mother goddess was known even during the Gupta period and the word Tantra is mentioned in the 5th Century texts as well as the Gangadhar inscription of the year 423 AD. But Tantra practices were kept secret and only came into the open in the 7th Century AD. Their most elaborate and vividly pictorial scriptures are the *Guhyasamaja, Manjushrimulakalpa, Sadhanamala, Nishpannayogavali,* and a number of other illustrated manuscripts, such as the *Prajnaparamita* and the *Pancharaksha.* Works similarly popular in the Himalaya were the *Chitralakshana,* a treatise on painting in the Indian tradition attributed to Nagnajit and the *Atreyatilaka* by the soothsayer Atreya. These scriptures contain instructions on the drawing of the images of Buddhist gods and goddesses and even of Brahmanical deities, such as Shiva, Uma, Karttikeya, etc. The hierarchy of the deities is also systematically classified for the benefit of the devotee because a Sadhana, or the detailed process of meditation through which spiritual eminence is said to be attained, was considered a psychic process for the visualisation and realisation of the deity with whom the worshipper identified himself. By means of certain Mantras, or verbal formulae, it was believed that the devotee could summon up a vast number of imagined deities, all of which were described iconographically in the Tantra scriptures. The magical instrument to compel deities to

reveal their spiritual attributes was the Vajra, a diamond or thunderbolt, and hence the name Vajrayana (vehicle of the thunderbolt).
Popularly known as Lamaism in the Himalaya, Vajrayana was based
on the class of rituals known as Sutras and Tantras, and these secret
practices in terms of art are intimately tied up with the great circle
of divinities, the magical diagram called a Mandala. A Mandala consists
of an important god and his entourage including divinities from the
whole pantheon of Buddhas, Bodhisattvas and Taras. At the apex of
this elaborate pantheon is the highest god, the Adi-buddha, to whom
five subordinate Dhyanl-buddhas (Pancha Tathagatap) owe their origin.
In the orbit of Vajrayana the convention of the duality of sexes was
developed with particular emphasis. Dhyana or meditation as abstract
thought was regarded as the male principle which remained inert until
activated by a cosmic female energy (Shakti or Prajna). Its hundreds
of different manifestations are seen in the Himalayan shrines, where
the Hindus have their eternal divine couples, Shiva-Parvati, Vishnu-
Lakshmi, etc., while the Buddhist shew several of their Yab-Yum
(father-mother) couples which are exuberantly frank, yet delicately
restrained symbolic representations. The function of the Vajrayana
images was essentially supernatural and the artists were prohibited
from making them unless they performed the liturgical rites of yogic
meditation on the divinity to be portrayed.

Vajrayana thought not only transformed the simple cult images of the
ascetic Buddha of earlier times by the inclusion of more occult
concepts, such as bejewelled and crowned Buddhas, but also caused
Buddha images to be vastly outnumbered by hundreds of gods and
goddesses (many of Hindu origin) which now joined the rapidly
expanding pantheon. The unrelenting process of deification turned all
objects, animals and even abstract conceptions into symbols of gods
and goddesses. Inevitably, in terms of art the emphasis shifted from
purity and refinement of form to iconography, even though the new
images were basically derived from Gupta canons. The stylistic progress
of art forms in the Himalaya was particularly retarded when the
famous Buddhist monasteries ceased supplying newer models of
Vajrayana images after the Muslim conquest of the Gangetic plains.
Because of this and also because reverence for canonical types was so
deeply rooted in the Himalayan regions, it is difficult stylistically to
distinguish works of art which were done at some point in the course
of hundreds of years after the 11th Century AD. The result was that
these standardised artistic forms, once introduced during a period of
political expansion or cultural and religious interchange, became more
or less permanently established in regional "groups" which depended
upon the origin of their models. These models were copied by generation
after generation, not because the artists could not do better, but
because in doing so it was believed that they accrued definite merit.
As well as predominantly Indian and Nepalese styles, these "groups"

included elements of Sassanian, Central Asian and Chinese art and even stylistic infiltrations from such far off places as the Baghdad school and the Mongol empire. The interchange of different elements of style did not always bring about a combination of forms and these groups mostly continued to exist side by side maintaining their individuality. This is the reason why Taranatha, the famous Tibetan historian, could still in the 17th Century AD distinguish the various Indian schools in the Himalaya even though these styles had disappeared in the Indian subcontinent since the Muslim conquest. In his *History of Buddhism* (1608 AD), he clearly identifies the Madhyadesha school (Pratihara art), the Eastern school (Pala art), the Old Western school (Gupta art) and the Kashmiri school. Taranatha's references to Nepal and Kashmir are interesting. He states: "In Nepal, the earliest schools of art resemble the Old Western school; but in the course of time, a peculiar Nepalese school was formed which in painting and bronze casting resembled rather the Eastern style. In Kashmir, too, there were in former times followers of the Old Western school of Madhyadesha; later on, a certain Hasuraja founded a new school of painting and sculpture which is called the 'Kashmir school'". Both these statements are in appreciable agreement with the known facts.

By about the 15th Century AD, the reverberations of this magnificent art tradition were also felt in Bhutan and Sikkim, where the people became more and more conscious of Vajrayana Buddhism and the mysteries of its art. The art of the great monasteries of eastern India, in the Gupta and Pala styles, was subjected to various influences in the different societies and cultures through which it passed (Ladakh, Central Asia and Tibet) on its long journey to Bhutan and Sikkim. These ideas and art prototypes finally arrived after about a thousand years, as if almost completing a full circle of the Buddhist prayer practice of circumambulation from the left to the right around the Stupa, the Himalaya. Bhutan and Sikkim thus had the opportunity to benefit from the varied elements originating from the art traditions of the Pala-Sena dynasty in Bengal and Bihar, the Gurjara-Pratihara kingdom further west, the Karkotas in Kashmir, the mannerists of Central Asia, the Abbasid and Chinese T'ang empires and finally Tibet with its magnificent specialised art. Appropriately called the art from "the western countries", a collective term by which the Chinese also described the regions of Central Asia and India, these pictorial elements, however, infiltrated Bhutan and Sikkim rather haphazardly. In an attempt to force innumerable and sometimes contradictory elements of style into their works, the artists with rare exceptions generally failed to impart that indescribable spiritual radiance which emanated from earlier examples of Buddhist art. The holy images of Bhutan and Sikkim, constructed unimaginatively and mechanically, express a cold religious dogma rather than a living divine ideal. The stress is primarily on the robes with their intricate embroideries and ornate floral motifs, details which are done with considerable skill. On the other hand, Bhutanese and Sikkimese artists display a great deal of mastery in depicting secular subjects such as the donors of the shrines. Their talent is similarly apparent in certain Tantric motifs projecting art as part of magic and ritual, seen particularly in Goinkhangs, rooms reserved for the inmates of the demoniac world. In this grotesque world of fantasy the artists apparently had a greater freedom of action than when modelling images of gods.

Bhutanese art is particularly rich in bronzes of different kinds which are collectively known by the name Kham-so (made in Kham), even though they are made in Bhutan, because the technique of making them was originally imported from the eastern Tibetan province of Kham. Wall-paintings and sculptures in these regions are basically formulated on the principal "ageless" ideals of early Buddhist art forms, even though their emphasis on details is derived from Tibetan models; their origins can easily be discerned, despite the profusely embroidered garments and glittering ornaments with which the figures are lavishly covered. In the religious sphere, Bhutan and Sikkim continued to follow the teachings of the saint Padmasambhava, founder of the "Red Hat" sect of Buddhism, who in the 8th Century AD with his wonder-working powers had firmly established Vajrayana Buddhism in Tibet. But in the 14th Century AD, in other Buddhist regions of the Himalaya, the new reform movement of the "Yellow Hat" sect had already taken hold of people's imagination. This movement, calling for a return to the Buddha's own teachings to sift genuine from apocryphal tradition, was initiated by noted religious reformes such as Buston (1290-1364 AD), Kumaramati (1349-1412 AD) and Tsongkha-pa (1357-1419 AD). At the same time, while this teaching about the purity of monastic discipline spread along the northern "grand route", a similarly popular movement propagated by Vaishnava reformers, based on beliefs in mysticism and all-embracing love, frequented the "great royal highway" in the south. Both these movements aiming at a return to the ancient fundamental tenets of religion, discarded ritualistic emphasis and sought to wean people away from the Shamanistic practices of medieval Indian civilisation.

The numerous rituals and their complicated symbols having thus become largely superfluous, in terms of art these movements focussed the artists' attention on basic art forms rather than the complicated icono-metry of Tantricism. Craftsmen, now less constricted by numerous and baffling iconographical details, created some of the loveliest wall-paintings to be found in the Himalaya. Essentially a projection of min-iature paintings onto the larger areas of walls, some exquisite exam-ples can still be seen in Ladakh, Nepal and the Siwalik ranges, epito-mising a new way of life as the route to the mysteries of aesthetic experience.

Although, as social movements, Hindu Vaishnava reforms as well as

BIRDS OF DIFFERENT VARIETIES FOUND IN HIMALAYAN MOUNTAINS.

Tsongkha-pa's "Yellow Hat" Buddhist sect were eventually stamped out by the combined forces of orthodoxy and feudalism, a new lyrical style in painting remained, of which the keynote was simplicity and human love. The preservation of this style in miniatures also owes its debt to Islamic monotheism and particularly to the mystic Sufism which the emperors Akbar and Shahjehan patronised when India was reunited under the Moghuls.

To sum up, Himalayan art is a crystallisation of the glorious tradition which probably began to take shape in the third millennium BC around the fertility symbols of the divine Yogi of the Himalaya, the Shiva prototype of the Indus valley civilisation. The Aryan semi-nomads took over the Indus valley symbols and infused into them the spirit of their gods of the elements. In the middle of the 3rd Century BC, when India was unified under the great emperor Ashoka, art forms tended more and more towards "realism" and eventually evolved into a definite style, as seen on the 2nd Century BC Buddhist monuments. The process of developing art produced a greater and greater variety of symbols and styles, especially after the image of the Buddha was invented in the 1st Century AD during the brief Kushan interlude of power. These art mannerisms, which reached their peak of perfection during the Gupta period, then began shaping the Himalayan art forms. The Gupta style embodied the best in both Hindu and Buddhist art and included in a broad sense the wonderful masterpieces of Ajanta cave painting. It became the main source of inspiration from which developed Indian medieval art (770-1200 AD), whose aesthetic motifs were adopted for Tantric spiritual experiences by peoples of different Himalayan regions. In this way, Himalayan art blossomed into varied styles which drew on the cultures of the Karkotas in Kashmir, the Gurjara-Pratiharas in the central Himalaya, the Pala-Senas in Nepal and on Tibet's artistic heritage as well as other Asian cultures. In the period that followed the 11th Century, these varied art styles continued to coexist while retaining their own peculiarities.

In the 14th-15th Century, out of the ruins of the medieval civilisation, there emerged new reform movements of popular mysticism both in Hinduism and northern Buddhism. In terms of art, excessive ritualistic symbolism and elaborate imagery were discarded, with the result that Himalayan art, especially that of the foothills, found new expression in a romantic, simple but highly expressive series of Pahari wall-paintings (16th-18th Centuries). They illustrate a remarkable synthesis of a mixed Muslim-Hindu-Buddhist culture which inaugurated a new era of secularism.

The visual diversity of Himalayan art—like the mountains themselves—is incredibly wide. The sculptures are carved in all forms of relief, and in painting the variety of colours is equally rich, like the lush Himalayan foliage. Yet, like the hundreds of gods and goddesses of the Hindu and Buddhist pantheons who aspire to the same divine ideal, these works of art express a magnificent unity in diversity. To find a *leitmotiv* for this fantastic art, therefore, one must look beyond its incidental stylistic, mythological, ritualistic and legendary associations, towards the majestic silver peaks symbolising primaeval ideals. In spite of infiltrations from or through western and central Asia, these dazzling, mighty barriers have sheltered and nourished inbred ideas and "timeless" symbols, creating a unified artistic tradition, epitomised by the symbolic pillar of the heavenly vault and the divine Yogi of the Himalaya.

In accordance with this theme, this volume attempts to provide an authentic pictorial record and a brief account of some of the almost unknown treasures of Himalayan art which have somehow survived the vicissitudes of time. This résumé of its historical and stylistic back-

BIRDS OF DIFFERENT VARIETIES FOUND IN HIMALAYAN MOUNTAINS.

ground is intended merely to convey the atmosphere, the least graphic of phenomena, and is not a comprehensive history of this vast subject. To quote the *Puranas*, scriptures of ancient India, "In a hundred ages of the gods, I could not tell thee of the glories of the Himalaya".

LADAKH

Ladakh, in the lap of the majestic, snow-covered Karakoram mountains, is a region of desolate valleys, unscaleable cliffs, almost impenetrable gorges and vast glaciers. With an average elevation of 5,300 meters, the Ladakh plateau occupies the north-eastern part of the Kashmir Himalaya. The great river Indus, rising from the springs of Sengge Khabab north of Manasarovara, enters Ladakh south-east of Demchok. Flowing in a north-westerly direction for about 560 kilometers in an asymmetrical valley, it then reaches the base of the Haramosh peak (7,397 meters) cutting the Ladakh range at Thangra and at Khartaksho, respectively south and north of Leh, the capital. With Haramosh on its right, the river once again cuts through a terrifying gorge, 5,200 meters deep, near Bunji, to flow for another 90 kilometers past Nanga Parbat. At the great bend of the river are Gilgit and Kohistan and beyond them Chitral. South of Kohistan between the Indus and the Swat, rivers which are fed by the glaciers and snow-fields of the towering mountain ranges between the Indus and the Hindu Kush, is Uddiyana, "the garden" of olden days, now called the Swat valley. To the north-east stretch the immense untrodden heights of snow and ice which form Ladakh's northern boundaries and separate it from Chinese Turkistan. Two important tributaries fed by the melting Karakoram glaciers join the Indus on its right bank, the Shyok at Khapula and the Shigar near the historic town of Skardu. On its left bank it is similarly joined by three rivers—the Zanskar, Dras and Astor—which are fed by the glaciers of the Great Himalaya. From Leh (3,300 meters) can be seen several magnificent peaks such as Masharbrum (7,803 meters), Gasharbrum (8,068 meters) and Chogori, also known as K2 (8,615 meters). Below the iceline of perpetual snow, these mountains form rugged, barren land masses which descend steeply into deep valleys through which extremely narrow green belts of vegetation follow lonely rivulets and streams. Apart from such sparse streaks of green, the spectrum is limited to the graduated greys and browns of the bare, barren hills which rise out of the flat stony high valleys spreading as far as the eye can see.

With an area of about 117,000 square kilometers, Ladakh's population is barely 88,000. The inhabitants live in small villages composed of mud huts at heights between 2,500 and 4,500 meters. These hamlets spread to the Nubra valley in the north and north-west, to the lofty uplands of Rupshu in the east, to Zanskar in the south and south-west, and towards the western towns of Kargil, Suru and Dras, which lie on the incredibly high road connecting Leh with the Kashmir valley.

As early as the time of the emperor Ashoka (273-236 BC), Buddhism is said to have been introduced to Ladakh through a missionary called Madyantika and his disciples. Such missionaries were deputed by the emperor himself, and, according to the Ladakh chronicles, "the holy men came with sacred books and spread the message of the Buddha beyond the Indus". It is known that Ashoka had also sent missionaries to Ceylon, Burma, Nepal and even to the Hellenistic kingdoms of the Mediterranean. After the disintegration of the gigantic Maurya empire (185 BC), whose advance post controlling the western Himalaya was under a viceroy residing at Taxila, this religious and artistic fertilisation was carried on by the Sunga and the Satavahana dynasties.

New ideas in art meanwhile emerged in north-western India, in the wake of the political and cultural tensions which followed the collapse of Alexander the Great's decrepit empire. Alexander had invaded the Punjab in 327-26 BC and his successors, the Seleucids, established themselves in north-western India, until they were ousted by the nomads of Central Asia. These nomads having no particular civilisation of their own, a syncretistic culture developed in the area which included Turkistan, Afganistan, Iran and the western Himalaya. These events were inevitably followed by indigenous political and cultural resistances in Iran and India, resulting in a consciously nationalistic culture under the Guptas in India and under the Sassanians in Iran. Even after the Gupta empire weakened under the onslaught of the White Huns, and the Sassanians finally collapsed before the Muslim Arabs, their tradistions for a long time to come continued to be followed in their respective areas of cultural influence.

Following the eclipse of the Greek empire, a brief interlude during which the Parthians and Sakas encroached upon Kabul, Kashmir and western Punjab is interesting because these nomads encouraged the art forms of the Hellenistic civilisation. But Indo-Hellenistic decorative and iconographical prototypes did not blossom in their new setting until about the turn of the century, when the Yueh-Chih driven out of their homes in Kansu by the Hsiung-nu (Huns?), established themselves in the valleys of the Hindu Kush, the Indus valley and the vast areas of north-western India.

They are known as the Kushans, and their outstanding ruler Kanishka became an ardent Buddhist and extended his authority at least as far as Mathura, where idols of the Buddha were made for the first time in the 1st Century AD. It is also believed that the image of the Buddha was perhaps made contemporaneously in Taxila under the patronage of the Kushans. In any case, the invention of Buddha's figure finally demolished the earlier anti-idol attitude of the faith which, with injunctions against the sensuous appeal of objects expressed in colours and shapes, had retarded the inventive genius of artists. It was certainly an advance from a system of formal intellectualism to a popularly-based religion giving added inspiration to the Bhakti movement, which preached the passionate attachment and loyalty of a devotee to a particular deity. In the Himalaya, where people were steeped in popular folk-cults, superstitions and ideas alien to the canonical teachings, the prohibition of idols was too abstract a concept to take root. Thus Kanishka's championship of Buddhism was greatly facilitated because, at the same time, the puritanism of Hinayana

A GODDESS OF ABUNDANCE, THIKSE MONASTERY, LADAKH. 15th—16th CENTURY AD.

THE BUDDHA, LADAKH.
5th—6th CENTURY AD.

THE BUDDHA, PHYANG MONASTERY,
LADAKH. 725—56 AD.

Buddhism gave way to popular tastes, and representational art began flourishing from the spread across the Himalaya of the Mahayana order.

The invention of the Buddha's image has the same cardinal importance for the history of eastern art as the first sermon of Gautama has for the Buddhist religion. This single aesthetic ideal became the focal point from which emanated thousands of stylistic variations illustrating the development of Asian art over a long period of many centuries. Among the first to receive the benefit of this new artistic ideal were the territories of the western Himalaya, because Mathura was an important mercantile and cultural centre which was joined by the "great royal highway" to the high roads from Central Asia via Taxila, and from the Indus valley through Minnagar. When its craftsmen created the Buddha's image, Mathura had already been a provincial capital of the Mauryas and the Sungas. Similarly, Taxila, where Buddhist sculpture in the Gandhara style was perhaps invented, was also a provincial capital under the Mauryas. It was the residence successively of Indo-Greeks, Scythians and the Parthian ruler, Gondaphares, and it continued to be an important trade and university town until it was destroyed in the 5th Century AD by the Huns.

The Mathura images of the Buddha, like the famous figure at Sarnath dedicated by the monk Bala, were basically derived from the massive indigenous sculptures of Yakshis, of the Maurya and Sunga periods. First seen on the Indus valley seals, Yakshis (spirits of nature and fertility) were depicted as super-human titans, together with other symbols such as the Nagas or serpents, in several early monuments of India. Inspired by the beautifully carved figures of Yakshis, such qualities as the sensually rounded limbs and the vigorous yet restrained poses, by which the body resting on either the right or the left leg produced marvellous outlines, were infused into the Mathura images; even the faces of the Mathura Buddhas, radiating a feeling of friendly warmth, recall the lovely, softly-smiling expressions of Yakshis. Following the ancient Indian practice, the drapery, with a conceptual stress on the seams and borders of the garment, was indicated by incised lines, thereby enhancing the softness and roundness of the flesh by a simple method of swelling, interlocking surfaces. Displaying all the Lakshanas (auspicious marks) that distinguish the body of a Buddha from that of an ordinary mortal, with broad shoulders and tiny waists, the Mathura figures of the master, in skill, sculptural quality and size were forceful projections of the Maurya and Sunga statues.

On the other hand, the Buddha image created directly under the patronage of the Kushans was first seen on Emperor Kanishka's gold coin, which is inscribed in provincial Greek "Boddo", probably an Iranian form written with Greek letters. The spectacular Gandhara style of the Buddha figure was a combination of various ideas and stylistic elements drawn from the pagan repertory of craftsmen from different countries, and the style approximated the late Hellenistic or Roman imperial art of the early centuries after Christ. Craftsmen and artists evolved a hybrid school in which the whole range of imagery was transplanted so that the Buddha appeared in robes displaying the

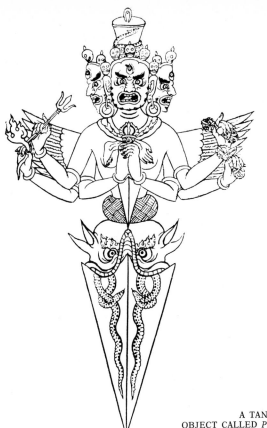

A TANTRIC RITUAL
OBJECT CALLED *PHURPA KILA*.

rhythmic, voluminous folds of Hellenistic or Roman pallium-like
garments.

The short-lived historical interlude of Kushan power is remarkable
because it brought about an interaction between different art styles
prevailing in the widely spread areas of its vast supra-national state.
This resulted in the development of several branch styles, some of
which were still in experimental stages when the patronage disappeared,
as suddenly as it had emerged. When the Sassanian victories weakened
Gandhara's contact with the Roman world, its art, too, gradually
declined after the 3rd Century AD. Instead, the Mathura sculpture
began to assert itself, and, in its ripe period, anticipated the sophisticated style of expression of Gupta art. But before giving their place
completely to the Gupta style, the Mathura examples had absorbed
several elements from the Gandhara models. In some of the art pieces
of this period, the folds of the garment were indicated (as precisely

47

described by Professor Benjamin Rowland Jr.) by means of "a schematic convention of quilted ridges falling in repeated loops down the median line of the body, so that the forms appear nude as seen through a network of cords".

The Guptas, an obscure dynasty at Pataliputra during the Kushan supremacy, gained power under Chandragupta I, who brought under his control Bihar, parts of Bengal and the Ganges plain. His successor Samudragupta (328-76 AD) conquered most of northern India and, having made Assam, Nepal and the Siwalik ranges his tributaries, campaigned aganist the western Indian satraps. The satraps were not, however, annihilated until the time of Chandragupta II (378-414 AD) whose influence reached beyoned the Hindu Kush. According to L. Petech, his authority was accepted even in eastern Iran, if Vahilika mentioned in one of his inscriptions should identify with Balkh (Bactria). Under Kumaragupta I (415-55 AD), the Gupta empire reached its political and cultural zenith, the splendour of which was a marvellous culmination and refinement of several techniques of earlier Indian art and forms of the Buddha's image. The Gupta sculptures, with their beautifully clear-cut and rhythmic surfaces, harmonious proportions and serene expressions, were based on the well-defined iconography of such works as the *Vishnudharmottaram* and the *Kamasutra*. Like the manuals of the Byzantine tradition, these established norms of aesthetic practice greatly facilitated the introduction of their forms in new areas such as the Himalaya.

The Buddha (page 45), recently discovered in Ladakh, is perhaps one of the earliest bronzes in the Gupta style in this area. Its transparent robe recalls some of the Gupta masterpieces of stone sculpture at Sarnath in which, by the 5th Century, unlike their Mathura counterparts, all traces of drapery folds had disappeared. The hair covering the head like a cap is made in the form of snail-shell curls, while the master is wearing a Sanghati (monastic robe) thrown over his left shoulder and covering his body down to the ankles. This sheath-like garment reveals the beautifully moulded limbs, giving an illusion of a nude figure. The simplicity and crystalline perfection of this essentially abstract conception has been marvellously achieved through the Gupta technique of gentle interlocking of predetermined balance to create the rounded fullness of form and the warmth of flesh. The pose, with the knee of the left leg slightly bent, has resulted in a marvellous gravitational and compositional balance. This style of lyrical beauty based on the simplified geometric purity of form is typically Gupta. Also in keeping with the Gupta tradition, the face is made according to a metaphorical method, by which the different features are moulded in imitation of suitable shapes in the world of nature. Accordingly, the face of this Buddha figure has "the countenance of a perfect oval of the egg, the eyes are shaped like lotus buds or petals; the lips have the fullness of the mango, and the brows the curve of Krishna's bow".

Yet, as with most figures of the Buddha made in different parts of Asia, the provenance of this figure can be more or less determined from the features which reflect the faces of original and ethnic groups of the local people.

Ladakh, bearing the imprint of a trade-route civilisation, during the Kushan period had already become one, if not the principal point through which models of Buddhist art forms from the Indian mainland were carried by way of at least three important trade routes to Khotan and Yarkand and other centres situated on the famous silk routes of Central Asia. The two great arches formed by the caravan routes along the northern and southern edges of the Taklamakan desert reunited at Tun-Huang in the east and at Kashgar, close to the Pamirs, in the west. Kashgar especially was an important junction which was also connected through Yarkand to Leh by way of the Karakoram pass. These routes were in turn connected to the great trade routes from India and China to Iran and Rome which passed through the Hindu Kush passes from Bactria to Taxila in Gandhara, consisting of the valley of the Kabul river, the Swat valley, and the Kashmir valley. Ladakh, therefore, naturally benefited from the commercial and cultural intercourse. Though the art forms in Kashmir by the 5th Century AD had become predominantly Gupta, a certain cultural admixture was inevitable with the local Iranian culture in Khorezm, Sogdiana and Bactria (Turkistan), and the mixed Graeco-Roman-Indian style in Afghanistan.

Apart from the actual models, particularly bronzes, the main "carriers" of Buddhist art prototypes were the Patas, on which painted models of the Buddhist pantheon were carried by the missionaries from one place to another to spread the message of their religion. The use of the narrative Pata was known from time immemorial in India, where a class of itinerant story-tellers called Mankhas or Saubhikas roamed from one place to another on occasions of feasts and celebrations. The Patas served as indispensable instruments of art-communication, especially in remote areas, such as Ladakh.

It was during this period that Central Asia freely absorbed the artistic achievement of the famous cave paintings of Ajanta in India. Even though these magnificent rock-cut temples were situated in the dominions ruled by the Vakataka dynasty, the pilgrims visiting this holy place of Buddhist legend apparently had easy access through the Gupta territories, especially after the marriage of Prabhavati, the daughter of Chandragupta II, to the Vakataka king Rudrasena. The frontiers of the Gupta empire being the immediate point of contact with the flourishing trade centres beyond the western Himalaya, and the main branch of the Gupta dynasty being paramount in the 5th Century, the stylistic influences of Ajanta are, in a broad sense, given the appellation "Gupta style".

It is now well established that the basic elements of Gupta style,

A COMBINATION OF THE EIGHT AUSPICIOUS EMBLEMS CALLED *TAGED-PUMZO*.

together with the influences emanating from the semi-classical school of Gandhara which flourished between the 1st and the 5th Centuries, primarily shaped the future evolution of art in Ladakh and Central Asia. The whole group of wall-paintings discovered at Miran on the southern caravan silk route are largely the product of this school. With the eastward spread of Buddhism along the silk routes, the iconography as well as several points of style peculiar to the early wall-paintings of Tun-Huang also owe their inspiration to this source. This relationship between early Central Asian paintings and the Gupta style and its later art forms in fact extended to the whole series of works of art from the north-eastern part of the Gandharan region called Ysufzai (by way of the route through Swat valley) to the southern track of the silk route spreading out to China. These art forms played an important

A VIEW FROM THE THIKSE MONASTERY, LADAKH.

part, especially in the middle years of the 7th Century AD which were marked by comparatively extensive contacts between Nepal, Tibet and China at a time when Ladakh played an important catalytic role.

The new stylistic elements of subtle sensuality and ease of line of the later Gupta period were transmitted to the Bodhisattvas and Taras in the 7th Century AD sanctuary of Fondukistan, just as this style gave its linear elegance to the painted niches at Bamiyan in Afghanistan. The influence of this style was also localised in the trade centres on the northern caravan route of the silk road from Tumschuq to Kucha, Agsu and Qarashahr, and left traces even in the art of Sogdiana and Chorasmia. Inevitably, however, in the process of interaction and fusion with the conventional Turkish, Kushano-Iranian and Romano-Sarmatian schools of southern Russia, much of the finesse and lyricism, as seen at Ajanta, was submerged beneath the heavy contours of darker colours. The only exception to this tendency towards heavy contours or bands of deeper pigments is found in the wall-paintings of Tun-Huang where, due to the close religious and political relationships between the T'ang empire and India at the thime, the softness of the later Gupta style and colour appear to have been imitated with greater fidelity and zeal. Unfortunately in Ladakh we do not have any examples of wall-paintings from this period. The difference between the elegant and varied styles of later Gupta art and the Asian paintings with deeply demarcated lines in darker colours can be compared if one looks respectively at **A Devotee** painted in the 11th to 12th Centuries (page 57) and **A Goddess of Abundance** (page 44) painted in the 15th to 16th Centuries. That we should skip a period of several centuries and yet see these valid stylistic comparisons may appear strange at first; but in the Himalaya, as in Tibet, it is no longer feasible after about the 11th Century AD to assign a work of art to a period, school or artist on the basis merely of distinguishing their manners or styles. Nor did geographical vicinity determine the style because the monastic studios entirely depended on models sometimes procured from distant centres of Buddhist learning and copied for hundreds of years. These standardised artistic forms became consolidated in "groups", so that attempts sometimes made to achieve a synthesis between different "groups" merely resulted in a sort of "welded" form in which each group could be easily distinguished. This joining together of groups of styles from various sources is seen in a most remarkable bronze recently discovered in the Phyang mona-stery in Ladakh. **The Buddha** (page 55), like most of the standing Buddhas, displays the common Abhaya-mudra (gesture of reassurance) but combines elements of styles borrowed from various sources. The manner of the folds of the garment falling over the torso clearly recalls the 4th-5th Century AD Buddhas of Mathura in which the robe combines the transparency of the Gupta school at Sarnat with the naturalistic treatment of Gandhara garments. The softly quilted folds thus formed are more like buffeted ropes in the form of loops sym-

THE BUDDHA, PHYANG MONASTERY LADAKH. 9th—10th CENTURY AD.

metrically hanging from the centre of the chest and spreading out towards the right and the left shoulders.

The squarish pattern of the loops over the stomach is akin to the style in some of the earliest known examples of Buddhist sculpture in Central Asia, a style which was also imitated in China in the 4th Century AD. The curious spiral folds on the arms, which seem to have no relevance to the naturally-falling folds of the Gandhara Buddhas, are

A ROYAL CAMP, ALCHI MONASTERY, LADAKH. 13th—14th CENTURY AD.

A DEVOTEE, ALCHI MONASTERY, LADAKH. 11th—12th CENTURY AD.

VISHNU BALARAMA, SWAT VALLEY, LADAKH. 8th CENTURY AD.

here identical to some of the 3rd Century AD wall-paintings at Miran; a beautiful detail from a painting showing a similar treatment of drapery over the arms is preserved in the National Museum in New Delhi. Then, abruptly, the sculptor has discarded this provincial style

58

A BUDDHA-SHAKTI, ALCHI SHRINE, LADAKH. 11th—12th CENTURY AD.

from the north and has made the lower part of the garment covering
the legs in the classical Gupta style. The transparent covering like a
wet cloth sticking to the body beautifully reveals the immaculate perfection of the thighs. The under-garments, just above the ankles,

MAHASARASVATI, ALCHI MONASTERY, LADAKH. 11th—12th CENTURY AD.

AN APSARAS, ALCHI MONASTERY, LADAKH. 11th—12th CENTURY AD.

again resemble more closely the Gandhara manner. The slanting half-closed eyes and the Urna are inlaid with silver which, combined with softly smiling lips, radiate a friendy warmth welcoming a devotee's adoration. This, in fact, is one of the individualities of the Kashmiri style, perhaps not a merit as it has a tendency towards slightly bloating the face. The profile appears to be construceted on a scheme of three lines; one plane includes the forehead and the nose, the second is a line from the tip of the nose to the point of the chin, which is practically touched by the lips, and the third section is a line reaching from the point of the chin to the neck. The jaw portion of the face from the ears down to the neck is oblong and a bit heavy. Nevertheless, the total effect imparts a distinctive character to the face, especially as the head is supported by broad shoulders. The torso is well-built and muscular and the waist narrow. Notwithstanding the tension created by all these different styles, this lovely bronze is strangely vital and graceful.

After the disintegration of the Gupta empire in the 6th Century AD, the inheritors of its art traditions included not only the later Guptas, but also Harshavardhana of Thanesar (606-64 AD), Yashovarman of Kanauj (c. 700-52 AD) and Lalitaditya of Kashmir, one of the greatest patrons of art to uphold this tradition. In the Kashmir valley, which had formed part of the empires of Ashoka, Kanishka and Mihiragula, had appeared a new local dynasty called the Karkotas, founded in 625 AD by Durlabhavardhana. The Karkota empire grew into a formidable power taking advantage of the crumbling empire of Harshavardhana, while the bitter struggle between Tibet and China, which started in 660 AD, gave it further opportunities for expansion. At the height of its power during the reign of Lalitaditya (725-56 AD), Karkota influence, according to Hermann Goetz, extended from Mysore to Mongolia and from Bengal and Orissa to Afhanistan. In any case, from this period onwards, Ladakh became closely integrated into the Kashmiri cultural orbit and its art forms were essentially moulded by Kashmiri styles. The oldest Karokta monuments are at Pandrethan. "the old capital", but the real founders of medieval Kashmiri art were Lalitaditda and his able chief minister, Chakuna. The latter originally came from Central Asia. These two patrons built the famous town of Parihasapura or Paraspor on the Srinagar-Baramula road, the great Sun temple of Martand, the Stupas of Pandrethan, the temples of Wangath (Bhutesar), Bunyar, Narasthan, Malot, etc. In this period, Kashmir also produced some very beautiful bronzes. One typical Buddhist bronze piece of this period in the classical Kashmir style is **The Buddha** (page 45), which is very closely related to another piece which is in the British Museum and is ascribed to Lalitaditya's reign by Douglas Barrett. In this magnificent sculpture, in which the Buddha is seen sitting in the Dhana-asana and Abhayamudra attitude, the end of his robe is elegantly carried over his left arm and softly indicated at the ankles and over

MANKHAS OR ITINERANT STORY TELLERS AT A FESTIVAL.

his left shoulder. The face of the Buddha is very similar to the types seen at Avantipur and especially at Masrur. The master is seated on a cushion laid on a throne supported by dwarf pillars, which are narrow with simple capitals, and similar to the wooden types seen in the Ajanta frescos. In between the pillars and flanked by two seated lions is a seated Atlas supporting the throne with his two arms symmetrically upheld. This Atlas figure does not appear in the art of Gandhara, but is characteristic of such monuments as the Stupa built by Chakuna in Lalitaditya's new capital at Parihasapura, about 10 kilometers from Srinagar. The only features roughly resembling the Gandhara art are the pillars and the lion-supported throne as well as the textile that covers it. But in Gandharan art the pillars are of entirely different form, while the lion and the pillar supports are never found together.

A DHARMAPALA, LAMAYURU MONASTERY, LADAKH. 15th—16th CENTURY AD.

Kashmiri stone sculptures of about this time also display close similarity to the style of this figure, reinforcing the view that Kashmiri art of the Karkotas had by the time of Lalitaditya practically shaken itself free from all the Gandhara influences. The struggle between the Gandhara style and the Gupta school of Mathura in the 4th and 5th Centuries AD was reflected as far away from the Indian borders as the Bamiyan valley in Afghanistan, where one can compare two colossal Buddha images cut out of gigantic rocks. The smaller of the two sculptures (38 meters) is chiselled in a style which roughly belongs to the early Gandhara type, while the larger Buddha (53.3 meters), with its drapery clinging closely to the body on a net of strings covered with Avalokiteshvara belonging to a later period, similarly carved in the clay, is clearly of Gupta inspiration. At Mulbek in Ladakh a figure of Kashmiri style, retains no influence of Gandhara whatsoever.

Lalitaditya's reign was the final flowering of a refined court culture, which claimed its origin from the 2nd Century AD with the advent of sophisticated classical Sanskrit culture. It was stimulated by the works of Kanishka's poet laureate Ashvaghosa; by the famous "Nine Gems", the greatest intellectuals in the court of Chandragupta II; by the eminent literati Bana, Mayura and Divakara and even by foreigners, such as Hsuan Tsang, who gathered round Harshavardhana. Against this background, iconographically, too, both Hinduism and Buddhism had undergone a far-reaching transformation. Both these religions assembled a multitude of deities by assigning special aspects to the leading gods, their females and attendants. The Hindu iconography of Karkota took over the pantheon of the Gupta period and made it even more elaborate. Here, the deity most venerated was the heavenly king Vishnu —riding the sun-eagle Garuda, sleeping as Narayana on the serpent Ananta, or sitting with Lakshmi his consort. His several incarnations, such as Krishna Vasudeva, the hero of the Bhagavata cult, Vishnu Balarama and the semi-animal forms of Varaha (boar) and Narasimha (man-lion), were increasingly depicted. The lyrical, quiet and marvellously balanced proportions of these sculptures are well represented by **Vishnu Balarama** (page 58). Balarama, who was the elder brother of the Hindu god Krishna, is seen here as an alternative incarnation of Vishnu as well as that of the great serpent Sesha. As such, he holds in his four arms the Padma (lotus), Shankha (conch-shell), Hala (ploughshare) and Musala (pestle). His elaborate crown consists of three symmetrical triangles from whose sides his hair falls in two long braids on to his shoulders and hangs behind his ears. His eyes are inlaid with silver and his lips with copper. The scarf, which in the Swat valley examples runs all over four arms, is here replaced by the snake whose long body symmetrically runs between the folded legs of the squatting figure and forms a semi-circle in front of the inverted lotus throne. This plait-work transformed into a long garland of snakes is found in late Gupta-Pratihara temples of north-eastern

JUGGLERS DOING TRICKS AT A FESTIVAL.

Rajasthan. Balarama's beautiful torso and narrow waist are bare except for the solitary necklace and the Ajina worn over his left shoulder. The sevenheaded hood of the snake against the combined halo and Vesica contribute to the perfection of balance and composition.

Kashmir's contribution to Hindu iconography based on Vaishnava and Shaiva theology became very popular all over the Indian sub-continent, where they were significantly said to have come directly from Kailasha, the mountain of gods. In Kashmir, a great centre of the Vuha cult, deities with three or more faces were depicted in several temples, for example on the western walls of the antechamber in the Martand temple during Lalitaditya's time (c. 725-76 AD).

In a parallel development in eastern India, the Vajarayana Buddhist pantheon of gods and goddesses also greatly expanded in fantastic forms

A SYMBOLIC REPRESENTATION OF YAMANTAKA, THIKSE MONASTERY, LADAKH.
15th—16th CENTURY AD.

at the great monastic institutions of Nalanda, Odantapuri and Vikra-mashila. Earlier phases of Mahayana Buddhism had already conceived the idea of Bodhisattva Padmapani, the future Buddha Maitreya and Avalokiteshvara. But later, under the influence of great patriarchs like Vasubandhu, Asanga, Nagarjuna and several others, metaphysical and scholastic Buddhist thought incorporated a host of new divinities. With the *Dinnaga* a school of logic developed so that Yogacharya philosophy brought Buddhism into close proximity to Hinduism. Vajrayana Buddhism then greatly expanded its pantheon of deities from the des-criptions in treatises such as the *Guhyasmaja Tantra* and the *Man-jushrimulakalpa*.

Until Lalitaditya's time, Kashmir's contact with the Buddhist centres in eastern India was mainly through pilgrims who continued to bring in increasingly new models of Buddhist gods and goddesses cast in bronze, sculptured in stone and painted on cloth. But in the 8th Century AD when Lalitaditya expanded his empire towards eastern India, Vajrayana gods and goddesses in Pala style seem to have secured a strong foothold also in Ladakh. The Kashmiri monarch, having van-quished the later dynasty of the imperial Guptas in Magadha (Bihar-Bengal), appears to have deported to Kashmir not only its last ruler, Jivitagupta. II, but also a number of craftsmen. According to the *Rajatrangini*, Lalitaditya in the same manner had brought to Kashmir several craftsmen and scholars when he took Kanauj in 733 AD. These cultural contacts enormously enriched the iconography of Kashmiri art, bringing about a remarkable fusion with that of Kanauj and Magadha. Reinforced in this way, Kashmiri style, combined with elements of earlier Kushan as well as late Kidara-Kushan motifs from the west, bequeathed to Ladakh a remarkable art tradition.

After Lalitaditya's death in about 760 AD, the Kashmiri style patronised by this dynasty maintained its hold under his successors. In 786 AD, Kabul was taken by a Muslim expedition and a few years later the indigenous Turki Shahi princes were superseded by the Hindu Shahi dynasty, founded by one Lalliya Shahi. In 870 AD, Lalliya Shahi was driven from Kabul by the Saffarid Ya'qub ibn Laith and settled down in a new capital on the right bank of the Indus at Udabhanda. In the valley of Kashmir, the Utpala dynasty restored the control of Kashmir over the Punjab and Afghanistan during the second half of the 9th and the first quarter of the 10th Centuries AD. During the Utpala ascendancy, Avantivarman is reputed to have commissioned a number of works of art soon after he ascended the throne in about 855 AD. The Utpalas were responsible for some lavishly decorated monuments, such as Avantipur, Patan, Pandrethan (stone temple), Bamzu, etc. A number of magnificent and unique bronzes depicting Vishnu in different forms, such as the Vishnu seated on Garuda (now in the Prince of Wales Museum in Bombay), are products of this time. This trend in post-Karkota styles was stimulated a hundred years later when king Kshe-

THE EIGHT AUSPICIOUS EMBLEMS.

magupta (950-8 AD) married Didda, the daughter of Simharaja of the
Lohara dynasty. Some beautiful sculptures were also dedicated by the
colourful Didda who, first as queen and then as regent for her sons
and grandsons, was *de facto* ruler of Kashmir for nearly half a century.
After Didda's death in 1003 AD, the brilliant tradition of Kashmiri
style flourished undisturbed during the time of kings such as Anantadeva (1028-63 AD)and Jayasimha (1128-54 AD), in whose reigns, according to the *Rajatrangini*, "works of art received special attention and
protection by the king, queen and the ministers alike".

The slow transition of style during the post-Karkota period can be seen
in at least two pieces in the Srinagar museum-king Shankaravarman's
brass frame for an image of the Buddha Avatara found at Devasar,
and the Bodhisattva Padmapani in a group with his Tara. Unfortunately, there are hardly any examples of wall-paintings of this period in
the Kashmir valley, so that it is not possible to trace the continuity
of painting in the same way as sculpure. But its reflections can still
be seen in the lovely wall-paintings in the monasteries of Lamayuru

PAINTED GARMENTS OF A BODDHISATTVA, ALCHI MONASTERY, LADAKH.
16th—17th CENTURY AD.

and Alchi in Ladakh and Tabo in the Spiti valley and also in a few shrines in western Tibet, such as the "Red Temple" at Tsaparang.

After the founding of Lhasa (about 650 AD), the east-west "grand route" became more and more frequented, because it connected the Kashmir valley and Lhasa and also linked the trade centres of the Indus valley with the settlements along the river Brahmaputra and the upper Sutlej valley. This famous caravan route started from Srinagar in Kashmir, led over the Zoji pass to Leh in Ladakh, to the sacred lake area, Shigatse and finally to Lhasa. Models of Kashmiri art prototypes travelled along the route to western Tibet, that is, the territory west of the Mayum pass called Zhang-Zhung. This area was independent of Tibet in the first half of the 7th Century AD and it was ruled by the Lig dynasty of Indian origin with Turki connections. According to the Ladakhi chronicles studied by L. Petech, culturally as well as linguistically Zhang-zhung remained tied more closely to India and Turkistan than to Tibet even as late as the 10th Century AD. The area thus formed a part of the orbit of Kashmiri art also including the mountain region stretching from Gilgit through Baltistan and Ladakh to the sub-Himalayan hill states. In the 10th Century AD, Kyide Nyimagoin, a descendant of a collateral branch of the old Tibetan dynasty, fled and established an independent state in west Tibet. In 930 AD, presumably after his death, this state was divided among his three sons. Ladakh, according to the biography of Atisha, was handed over with full powers to Palgyigoin. According to Ladakhi chronicles, the sixth ruler in this line as given the Sanskrit name Utpala, and ruled from about 1080 to 1110 AD. Lhachen Utpala was a firm and enlightened ruler, who consolidated the Buddhist cultural heritage, as is evident from the magnificent monastery of Alchi.

In this shrine there are groups of paintings belonging to different periods. Some of the earliest paintings are in a chapel, whose marvellous **Altar** (page 49) is a colourful monument of the post-Lalitaditya Kashmiri style. Being a natural evolution from later Gupta mannerism and early Indian medieval art, it retains a perfect balance and harmony of the design as a whole. At the same time, the various details of the tendrils, flowers, animals and human figures have undergone a remarkable elaboration and re-interpretation. The whole wall is covered with a fantastic wealth of ornaments, twisting yet symmetrical tendrils among which are seated slim and elegant goddesses such as **A Buddha-Shakti** (page 59). The elaborately painted columns on the right and the left of the principal deity each support a Makara which is again stylised into tendrils dissolving into mushroom-like flowers. In fact, every decorative motif sprouts into a minor ornament, and every figure into masses of jewellery, symbols and attendants. The branches are rounded into the shape of medallions and in these arches of exuberant leaf scroll-work are placed dancing Apsarases and Gandharvas playing their instruments as they merrily point their flutes towards the main goddess.

The altar is seething with baffing details and yet on the whole has a soothing, balanced rhythm. Its restless dynamism, over-elaboration, intermeshed yet open form and strange playful light-heartedness is typical of the picturesque Alchi wall-paintings reproduced in this volume. A most beautiful detail from the murals in this chapel is **Mahasarasvati** (page 60). Sarasvati was the name of an ancient river, which disappeared in the Indian desert of Rajasthan. It was on the banks of this river that the Vedic Aryans composed many hymns and they deified the river as close up, the goddess of learning. During the Tantric age this Hindu goddess was also incorporated in the Buddhist pantheon, in which she appears in a number of forms. As Mahasarasvati she is usually shown sitting on the new moon resting on a white lotus. In this painting, which is closer to the Hindu version, the goddess, "resplendent like the autumn moon", sits on a swan, stylised in the shape of a stool, while the moon on the lotus is shown in the background. In one hand she holds the Vajra indicating her allegiance to Vajrayana. This marvellously sensuous goddess with her soft rounded breasts, the sweeping curves of her narrow hips, the gestures of her hands and the elegance of her poise has the distinctive features of the Kashmiri school. The delightfully transparent blue and brick-red backgrounds against which the lovely slender figure is portrayed produce an effect of partial depth and relief. The plasticity is enhanced by the skilful application of colours—yellows, greens, blues and reds—which are ably graded with clear transparent highlights producing the intended chiaroscuro effect. There is no trace of plumpness or fullness of the type seen in Bengali and Nepalese art. On the contrary, the Kashmir style has a well-defined preference for elegant, erect yet supple postures in which the measured undulation of the body with a slight upward tilt of the head has replaced the classical Tribhanga (pose of three bends). This contrasting combination of classical naturalism in modelling well-shaped limbs and stylistic angularity in the drawing of the garments, meticulously filled with squarish patterns of embroidery, is the chief characteristic of this style. The charming method of drawing the second eye projecting out of the profile line of the half-turned face is also typical.

Another interesting example belonging to the same stylistic group is the elaborate painting of **Vasudhara** (page 25). Evidently done by the sensitive hands of the master craftsmen of Kashmir who are even today known for their expertise, the painting shows meticulous designs of flowers and exquisite patterns. It is a true expression of the Kashmiri school, as has been largely substantiated by the copies of *Prajnaparamita* illustrated manuscripts which G. Tucci discovered in the ruins of upper Toling and which point to similar techniques of drawing and colouring. In this painting the Alchi artists have succeeded in focussing attention on the figure of the goddess herself, despite the glittering ornaments and trinkets and overwhelming embroidered garments which she wears. The figure appears to come out of the backdrop of halos, superimposed over practically a one-way traffic towards Tibet. But a certain interchange of ideas was, however, taking place through three trade routes on Ladakh's northern and eastern borders across the Karakoram ranges. Among these influences vague hints from the style called the Baghdad school, which was localised in the caliphal seat of the Abbasids, had already penetrated some art forms in Ladakh, though, naturally, these were the mixed product of several—and often opposing —influences. At Alchi, curiously enough, these influences are reflected in a solitary painting, **A Royal Camp** (page 56), which is with several paintings in the Kashmiri style. A Royal Camp seems to portray one of the subjects which are seen in the orbit of the Baghdad school. These were the illustrations to the *Makamas* of Hariri, portraying (in a style recalling the figures of shadow plays) the unscrupulous vagabond Abu Zayd, which became very popular in the first half of the 13th Century AD and had grafted a combination of the Chinese, Sassanian and Indian traditions of Central Asia on to the native cultures of the countries they conquered. In 1200-1230 AD, when one of Utpala's successors, Trashigoin, ruled in Ladakh, the great Mongol emperor Genghis Khan had brought under his control large areas from northern China and Iran to the Turkish-Mongolian territories, and was already knocking at the door of Ladakh from Turkistan across the Karakoram. In any case, this painting is as intriguing as the 6th-7th Century AD wall-painting in cave I at Ajanta, commonly known as the Persian Embassy, which depicts figures bearing resemblances to the people of Turkistan and other regions of Central Asia, with which Ajanta was apparently in contact at that time through the Sakas of Saurashtra and Malwa. The establishment in 1339 AD of a new dynasty in Kashmir by Shah Mir of the Swat valley did not disturb Ladakh's basic economic and cultural pattern established during Utpala's rule. The new Kashmiri rulers were too occupied in consolidating their domestic authority against the threat of the Tughlak dynasty at Delhi and the Mongols in the north. Ladakh luckily also escaped the destructive invasion of north-western India by Timur of Samarkand, who marched through Afghanistan to India at the close of the 14th Century AD. Towards the east also, the Mongol supremacy there having declined, Tibet was the centre of the struggle between the two families of the Rinpung-pas and the Phagmotru-pas. Thus, Ladakh left to itself, stabilised its socio-religious community under the ruler Trakbumde (1410-40 AD), and a number of new monasteries were built at important locations along the trade routes.

Trakbumde appears to have been greatly helped by a new movement of reform of Vajrayana Buddhism founded by Tsongkha-pa (1357-1419 AD). Known as the "Yellow Hat" sect, it called for greater purity of discipline and preached the importance of the basic monastic rules of Indian Buddhism. This reformed school made a complete reappraisal

KODALIPA, THIKSE MONASTERY, LADAKH. 1555—75 AD.

of the magical practices based on gnostic Tantric texts and reasserted the primacy of the fundamental and simple tenets of the Buddha's message. Like the conformist Tibetan king, Ralpa-cen (died 836 AD), who had proscribed any activity which did not follow the accepted Indian type in Buddhist art or literature, Tsongkha-pa's followers, too, promoted the cause of Sanskrit civilisation. Even works in Sanskrit which had nothing to do with Buddhism became popular, among them Kalidasa's famous poem *Meghaduta* (cloud messenger).

This reformation of religion also brought about a change in the subject-

GODHARA, THIKSE MONASTERY LADAKH. 1555-75 AD.

matter of the works of art, so that the emphasis once again shifted, as in early Buddhist art, to depictions of scenes from the Jatakas and legends of the story of the Buddha. One beautiful example of this at Alchi is **Scenes from the Buddha's Life** (pages 28-9). Here, in a single whole, various consecutive events of the life of the Buddha are depicted within panels which are demarcated by alternately-painted red and blue backgrounds. The figures, displaying a tendency towards elimination of plasticity and naturalism, are reminiscent of the Kashmiri wood sculptures. These drawings resemble the style of the west Indian school,

AN ATTENDANT OF YAMANTAKA, THIKSE MONASTERY, LADAKH.
15th—16th CENTURY AD.

as seen in the *Kalpasutra* manuscript, illustrated and written in Mandu
in 1439 AD (now in the National Museum, New Delhi), except that here
there is still a halfeh arted attempt at shading to produce a sort of
rudimentary depth and perspective. This has resulted in a curious
pattern of block-like squarish highlights. The overall impression is,
nevertheleess, attractive and the humans, animals, leaves and flowers
are arranged in a pleasing design of colourful squarish and triangular
spaces.

80

SHOPKEEPERS AND THEIR CLIENTS.

In these paintings there is no attempt at realism, a tendency which could be seen in the sculptures of western India as early as the 8th Century AD. If we compare in sequence the successive development of mannerism seen in the illustrated manuscripts of western India, the style in which the Scenes from the Buddha's Life are done fits in well. In the earliest surviving illustrated manuscripts and covers of the west Indian school belonging to the early 12th Century, the style is clearly seeking for expression through purely linear means even though an attempt is made to produce a sort of rudimentary modelling through tenuous grading and wash of colour. By the end of the 13th Century, attempts at modelling disappear so that plasticity and movement are conveyed by the sureness and expressiveness of line. They are also achieved by the stance of the figures and the disposition of their drapery.

THE DREAM OF MAYA DEVI, HEMIS MONASTERY, LADAKH.
EARLY 17th CENTURY AD.

A further stage was reached in the 15th Century development of style
as seen in the *Kalpasutra* and *Kalakacharya Katha* manuscripts (now
in the Prince of Wales Museum, Bombay). And it arrived at its logical
zenith in the 16th Century Mewar illustrations to works such as the
Chaurapanchasika, Bhagavata Purana and *Gita Govind*.

By the middle of the 15th Century AD, although most communities in Ladakh subscribed to the "Yellow Mat" sect, its reformed tenets again relapsed into the ancient ideas of the "Red Hat" beliefs. In a situation similar to the time of the White Hun attacks against the Gupta empire, people now put their faith in gods in their demoniac aspect who would protect them against danger. Their belief in the protector deities, such as Dharmapalas (defenders of the law), was, therefore, strengthened. In fact, the 100 years that followed Trakbumde's death (about 1440 AD) could not have been worse for Ladakh. It found itself in midst of the holocaust of wars and invasions, the futile vandalism and purposeless effacement of wall-paintings and destruction of sculpture, which had become common in the Indian subcontinent and Central Asia. During the time of Lotroi-chogden (1440-70 AD) Ladakh had accepted the sovereignty of the Kashmir valley, but this did not save it from raids from the valley especially after Lotroi-chogden was dethroned in 1470 AD by Lhachen Bhagen Namgyal (1470-1500 AD), a prince from a collateral branch of the family. In 1418 AD, Hasan Khan of Kashmir again raided Ladakh, and by the end of the century, it was threatened from the north. This time it was the Mongol Abu Bakr, the Khan of Kashgar, who, having conquered Gilgit and Baltistan, made many raids into Ladakh. It was not until 1517 AD that Ladakhi defenders under the leadership of Tashi Namgyal defeated the Mongol armies and killed their leader, Mir Mazid.

During this period, some very interesting sculptures in clay of the Dharmapalas were made. Some of these can be seen in the old and small monastery of Lamayuru which is on a steep slope about 200 meters below the main monastery. Dharmapalas are worshipped either singly or in groups of eight, and are said to wage merciless war against enemies of the religion. **Mahakala Bhattaraka** (page 65) is the Buddhist parallel of the Hindu deity Mahakala. He is blue in colour, has three eyes and terrible bare fangs. Like his Hindu counterpart, he is short, pot-bellied and decked in ornaments of snakes, skulls and tiger skins. In the lonely monastery of Lamayuru, he is seen defending the Stupa. **A Dharmapala** (page 64) is evidently another ferocious protector of the faith (he is not identified). According to the legend, the Indian saint, Padmasambhava, after he had vanquished all the malignant spirits in Tibet, invited those who promised to become Dharmapalas to join the Buddhist pantheon.

The most ferocious and iconographically complicated of the Dharmapalas is Yamantaka, the emanation of Manjushri. He presides over the eastern direction with a number of assistants who are assigned attributes similar to those of their chief. **An Attendant of Yamantaka** (page 80) is probably Chhogyal, who is the commander of Yamantaka's army. His colour is blue but he has one bull-head instead of Yamantaka's three. The origin of the bull-head is ascribed to the tradition which speaks of a holy man who lived in a cave, practising meditation. As he

SUDDHODANA CONSULTS A SIDDHA, HEMIS MONASTERY, LADAKH.
EARLY 17th CENTURY AD.

was about to achieve his objective and enter Nirvana, two thieves with
a stolen bull entered the cave and slaughtered it. When they saw the
ascetic, a witness to their crime, they beheaded him too. But to their
astonishment, the victim lifted the head of the bull and, replacing his
own head with it, became the ferocious form of Yama. He then not

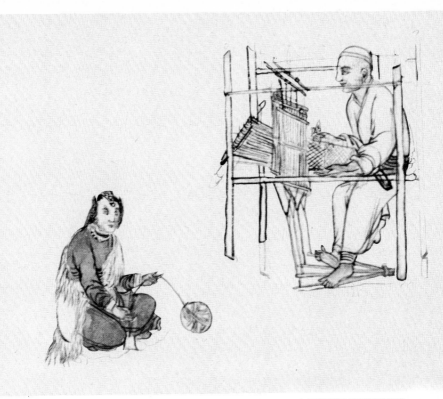

A HANDLOOM WEAVER.

only devoured the two thieves, but his insatiable thirst for human
blood threatened the whole population. The followers of the Vajrayana,
therefore, appealed to Manjushri who, then assuming the fierce bull-
headed form of Yamantaka, defeated Yama in a fearful struggle.
The Vajrayana pantheon revolves round Pancha Tathagata or what are
popularly known as the five Dhyani buddhas. *Sadhanamala* states:
"The Jinas (victorious ones) are Vairocana, Ratnasambhava, Amitabha,
Amoghasiddhi and Akshobhaya. Their colours are white, yellow, red,
green and blue, and they exhibit the Bodhyangi (teaching), Varadha
(boon), Dhyana (meditation), Abhaya (protection) and Bhumisparsa
(earthtouching) gestures of hands respectively". It was Sarvagyanami-
tra in the 8th Century AD who introduced Stotras (eulogistic hymns)
as a means of obtaining divine grace so that the artists began to

85

A CHANAK EAGLE, THIKSE MONASTERY, LADAKH, 15th—16th CENTURY AD.

depict in images the postures, ornaments and emblems of the principal
gods. The Dhyani buddhas thus became the embodiments of the five
Skandas or cosmic elements. These are Rupa (form), Vedana (sensa-
tion), Samjna (name), Samkara (conformation) and Vijnana (conscious-
ness). In fact, in this way, the five Dhyani buddhas merely conven-
tionalised the Tantric view of the world, the form of many sets of
fives—such as colours, directions, gestures, types of wisdom, types of
evil, components of personalities, families, family symbols and so on.

A YAK, THIKSE MONASTERY, LADAKH. 15th—16th CENTURY AD.

The unrelenting process of deification turned all objects—the cosmic principles, letters of the alphabet, directions and even emotions and desires—into symbols of gods and goddesses. Ten directions, eight kinds of hair-dressing, several kinds of protections, dances, musical instruments, four kinds of light, important animals were all deified, and even the abstract conceptions of Dana (charity), Maitri (love) and Gyana (knowledge) were transmuted into symbols. Artists depicting Tantric motifs, faced with the impossible task of reproducing these inexhaustible forms, seem to have invented an ingenious method of "dismantling" and then "binding" these elements together. This method synchronised with the basic Tantra premises of a number of separate elements manifesting themselves together in "streams" to form transitory phenomena, objects and shapes. Works which we consider complete pictures such as **Chanak Eagle** (page 86) and **A Yak** (page 87) are in Tantric terminology merely symbolic representatives of Yamantaka and therefore have meaning only as such. In Tantric art the two most important elements were known as Prapti (pertaining) and Aprapti (non-pertaining), as these served as the cohesive and disintegrating forces respectively. Homogeneity in these streams of elements was considered different from unity and termed the element of Nikayasabhagata. Every element by its very nature manifests itself just momentarily so that the whole of existence is like the changing effects produced by a kaleidoscope. One such marvellous vision is the **A Symbolic Representation of Yamantaka** (page 68). Here, a variety of elements coalesced by the Prapti element have produced a symbolic representation which is comprehensible to the initiated; yet, in keeping with Tantric norms, the manifestation is illusionary as the different interchangeable elements forming the picture are subject to the tensions exerted by the contradictory element Aprapti. These elements seem to radiate from the centre, always ready to disintegrate and fly out and then coagulate into new symbolic form. In this transitory, ever-changing process Nikayasabhagata (homogeneity) is never lost. This is graphically depicted in **A Tantric Manifestation of Symbols** (page 69). The scattered elements have an individual symbolism of their own as they float in space groping for new meanings and higher symbols.

In the sphere of Tantric art we are confronted with one of the richest mines of colour and line symbolism, undoubtedly inspired by treatises such as the *Vishnudharmottaram*. According to this Gupta treatise on painting, written in Sanskrit, each Rasa or emotion had to be painted in its expressive colour. With some variations, this principle was adapted by Vajrayana and a Tibetan work of the 11th to 12th Century AD, the *Manikabum*, assigned symbolic colours to each of the six syllables of *"Aum Mani Padme Hum"*, a Sanskrit Mantra repeated by every Buddhist to avoid rebirth in the six worlds depicted in the Wheel of Existence. Aum is white. Both in Buddhist and Hindu symbolism white represents heavenly purity and bliss. Ma is blue, being the colour of Asuras (demigods). The colour of Ni, which represents the human state, is yellow, like the robe of an ascetic. The animal state is depicted green, which is the colour of the syllable Pad. Me, symbolising the state of goblins, is red. Hum is given the colour black, which is the state of devils.

These paintings can hardly be compared with examples of abstracts of our own time, because of the important difference that formal higher values are achieved not merely by reducing or eliminating association

A DEVOTEE CONSULTS HIS GURU OR SPIRITUAL TEACHER.

with the human figure but by giving a precedence to initiate experience (Yoga) over mere knowledge. Tantra artists attempted to create visions and not images by seeking to translate knowledge into inwardly experienced drama where Prajna or gnosis is in the centre of the stage. The defeat of the Mongol Mir Mazid did not end the misfortunes of Ladakh, which faced even greater danger in 1532 AD when Abu Sayed Mirza, the new Khan of Kashgar, crossed the Sugat and Karagoram passes into Ladakh and in alliance with the Kashmiri prince, Sikandar, defeated Tashi Namgyal who was eventually executed by the Mongols. If it were not for the flexible manner in which the Buddhist monastic system played its central role, the complex of Ladakh's art and culture could not have survived the preceding century. In fact, in the course of

TSAMARIPA, THIKSE MONASTERY,
LADAKH. 1555—75 AD.

KUKURIPA, THIKSE MONASTERY,
LADAKH. 1555—75 AD.

just over two decades (1555-75 AD), Tashi Namgyal's nephew, Tshewang Namgyal, taking advantage of the temporary weakness of Ladakh's neighbours, quickly recovered and even re-asserted suzerainty up to the Mayum pass in the east and Baltistan in the west. Tshewang Namgyal is reputed to have rebuilt most of the religious institutions destroyed during the attacks of the past century and made them even more resplendent. In this mission the monasteries of Ladakh apparently benefited greatly from a number of craftsmen who, due to lack of work and uncertain tolerance in the neighbourhood, emigrated to Ladakh in search of employment.

The lovely wall-paintings in the famous monastery of Hemis depicting the life events of the Sakya Sage are said to have been painted under

KALAPA, THIKSE MONASTERY,
LADAKH. 1555—75 AD.

BHANDEPA, THIKSE MONASTERY,
LADAKH. 1555—75 AD.

the supervision of art masters from Kashgar, Khotan and Kashmir. The
Khotani painters had already won great fame in China at the beginning
of the T'ang dynasty. The works of art at the Hemis monastery, which
was founded by Senge Namgyal in 1602-6 AD, are stylistically remarkable, as they were done in a manner essentially inspired within the
sphere of the reformed ideas of Tsongkha-pa even though it is a Drukpa
monastery. **The Great Renunciation** (page 93) depicts the Gautama's
moving renunciation of the worldly life. There was feasting and dancing
and music, rich food and much revelry on that fateful evening when
the Sakya prince decided to become a mendicant. When everyone was
sleeping, he roused Chandaka, his faithful groom, and rode away on his
favourite horse, Kanthaka, without even saying farewell to his wife

and newly-born son. Once away from the city, Gautama cut off his beautiful flowing hair, stripped off his jewellery and his royal garments and sent them back to his father by the hand of Chandaka. This exquisite painting has effectively captured the atmosphere of the Great Renunciation scene. Kanthaka's grief of which he later died and the weeping Chandaka are marvellously portrayed against the background of associated legends. One of these depicted in the background shows a Naga (serpent) receiving perhaps the sacred book the *Prajnaparamita*, which is said to have been kept in safekeeping by the Nagas until such time as the human race was prepared to receive it. (The origin of Naga worship, according to tradition, was Kashmiri. When Hsuan Tsang entered the valley, he learnt of the belief that a member of Gautama Buddha's family had married a daughter of a serpent king. Many legends tell of the Buddha's birth when the Nagas gave him his first bath, and how later they became his disciples. It was also a serpent king, Mucilinda, who protected the Buddha from the god of evil, Mara, when he tried in vain to prevent him from achieving enlightenment.) The deity who, according to mythology, received Gautama's hair and the one who came disguised as a hunter and exchanged his soiled clothes with Siddhartha's royal garments, are also shown with other gods making offerings at this auspicious occasion. The flow of line, the scheme of colour as well as the facial types are very similar to some of the 10th Century AD paintings on silk from Tun Huang indicating that central Asian craftsmen may also have come from the eastern end of the Taklamakan desert. This stylistic analogy is particularly noticeable in **The Dream of Maya Devi** (page 82). According to this story, Gautama's mother Maya Devi dreamt of a white elephant entering her body from the right side. The king at once summoned an assembly of dream-interpreters who proclaimed that "the child of her womb will assuredly be a holy child and grow up to achieve perfect wisdom". In this painting the lyrical drawing and colouring and the solemn and dignified atmosphere make a picture of profound peace and tranquillity. The sparing use of golden lines and their judicious application reject any hint of the gaudiness which was so prevalent in many paintings of this period. Another most interesting painting in this group is **Suddhodana Consults a Siddha** (page 84). It depicts an episode of Gautama's life which is essentially of Vajrayana significance and was obviously improvised at a much later period. It shows Gautama's father consulting a Tantra master and his female partner. The Siddha is seen here being introduced by Suddhodana's minister Mahanama. The ideal link between Shivaite Tantras and Vajrayana on an intimate level is the group of 84 Mahasiddhas, who are the most eminent esoteric personalities of medieval India. The tales of the magical powers they acquired and their disregard for conventional morality are in keeping with their biographies from which ultimately all Tantric Buddhism is known as Mahamudra, by the practice of which any person irrespective

92

of caste, creed, sex or age could attain salvation if guided by the Siddhas.

Paintings and sculptures of the Siddhas are found in almost every monastery in the Himalaya. In the 16th Century AD, however, as the ties binding the craftsmen to ancient precepts loosened, the artists apparently found more elbow room to display their individual talents. A degree of relaxation of the ancient Indian tradition of artists' anonymity is also evident from a number of names of the painters which now appear below some of the paintings. To paint or make sculptures being an act of worship, the names of the artists sometimes recorded along with their patrons were intended to perpetuate acts of piety rather than recognition of their talents. "Through the merits thus earned", state some of the dedications, "may the donor with his kin obtain the state of Buddhahood". But now the artists' skill in "putting the colours together" is also mentioned. At the monastery of Thikse, names of Tondup Gyatso from the village Matto, Lobsong Tondup of Phyang, Dorjiskyab of Alchi, Tondup Namgyal from the village Spituk and many others are all written below their paintings in the nunnery chapel attached to the main shrine. These commemorative inscriptions also indicate a well-established school of Ladakhi painters who were apparently not permanently attached to particular monasteries, but travelled from place to place depending upon the demand for work. Nevertheless, the purpose of works of art continued to be essentially that of earning religious merit and, therefore, they did not basically vary from the laid-down precepts required by the patrons. This is demonstrated by some brilliant strokes of drawing and colouring in the following seven paintings of the Siddhas which are among a complete set of 84 Siddhas depicted in the courtyard of the main shrine at Thikse. **Tsaluka** (page 75) was a lazy individual who was disowned by society, because he was fond of sleeping. Therefore he lived in a cemetery, and at last he met a Yogi, who told him to "imagine that you draw all the phenomenal objects into your spiritual self, then meditating on an ocean, perceive that your awareness floats on the water like a duck". Tsaluka, despite his laziness, thus attained perfection and entered Nirvana in his lifetime. **Kodalipa** (page 78), a south Indian farmer, was digging the ground to rebuild his house when Guru Shantipa (who was on his way back from Ceylon) stopped to enquire what he was doing. Kodalipa explained that "selfish kings fight and render many people homeless. So I have to rebuild my house". Shantipa then told him that it as not enough only to rebuild his house unless he also rebuilt his attitude. He added, "First respect your teacher, realise that pain and pleasure spring from your own mind and learn to meditate on your primordial mind. Then dig out the roots of delusion that defile the mind with your sharp hoe, which is your inspired pure wisdom". Kodalipa gratefully received the message and after twelve years of meditation earned perfection. **Godhara** (page 79), a fowler by profession, hated his work because he disliked killing animals. One day by chance he came across a Yogi who told him to become a Buddhist and stop destroying living beings. He also taught Godhara to meditate at every dawn by concentrating on the songs of the birds and identifying himself with them. According to the legend, Godhara freed himself from the sin of killing animals during his life. **Tsamaripa** (page 90) was a cobbler who lived at Vishnu Nagar in eastern India. He attained the state of Siddhi after a Tantric teacher taught him how to practice meditation even while he was working. Tradition has it that while he meditated Vishvakarma himself came and assisted him to make shoes. **Kukuripa** (page 90) was a Brahman who became a Yogi. Once when he was on his way to Lumbini, he found a stray puppy and took care of it for twelve years before he went to heaven. The gods entertained Kukuripa lavishly but he was unhappy without his pet. So he came back to earth and, as soon as he touched the dog, she was transformed into an angel. She then taught him the Tantras of Prajna (knowledge) and Upaya (method) and thus both achieved salvation. **Kalapa** (page 91) was a very handsome man, so that, envious of his appearance, his colleagues disliked him. Disillusioned with life, he decided to renounce the world and took refuge in a cemetery. Here he met a Yogi who initiated him into the mysteries of Tantricism so that he could visualise the figure of a deity and then erase it at will from his memory. In this way he was able to bring under control the subject-object concept and achieve Nirvana in his lifetime. **Bhandepa** (page 91) who lived in the sky was once so amazed to see a monk flying in the air that he enquired of Vishvakarma who he was. He was told that the person he saw was an Arhat, a Yogi who had freed himself from delusion. Bhandepa, to become an Arhat, sought rebirth on earth and received religious instructions from Nakpopa. He practised friendliness, equanimity and compassion for a hundred years and thus earned salvation along with his four hundred followers.

These delightful drawings are said to have been done under the patronage of Tshewang Namgyal (c. 1533-75 AD), during whose time the two decades from 1555 to 1575 AD witnessed a remarkable consolidation of the monastic system. Having withstood the dark events of the previous century, Ladakh sent expeditions against both Guge and Baltistan. But this situation was short-lived and after Tshewang Namgyal's death, his weak successors could not hold on to their gains. Senge Namgyal (1595-1645 AD) made an effort to retrieve the position, but his attempts to capture Baltistan were thwarted by the Moghuls whose interest in Ladakh by this time had become too deep. In fact, since Babur's capture of Delhi in 1526 AD, a number of missions and expeditions with Moghul support had been sent to Ladakh. However, il was not until after 1585 AD when the great Moghul emperor Akbar established his rule in the Kashmir valley that Ladakh became a *de facto* part of the Moghul empire.

Under these influences (as in the Siwalik ranges) a change of style in painting took place in Ladakh. The actual process of its evolution is not clear but it is reasonable to assume that this development followed conditions identical to those which produced the marvellous Pahari miniatures. Some lovely examples of this style are seen painted on the loincloth of a Bodhisattva figure, over five meters high, at Alchi. Massive statues of the Buddhist deities in clay are found all over the Himalaya. The technique was apparently derived from eastern Turkistan where quarried stone did not exist. These clay figures were then painted with bright colours and the draperies decorated with flowers and designs and sometimes, as at Alchi, with different scenes from mythology and contemporary life. The drawing on the **Painted Garments of a Bodhisattva** (page 72) were done at a period much later than the making of the statue itself and are apparently painted on top of an earlier layer of paintings. The Bodhisattva's loin cloth reveals a fantastic world of designs depicting wonderfully varied scenes and employing the entire spectrum of brilliant colours. It is a symbolic whirlpool and an extraordinary record, as it were, of the turmoil of wars, invasions and upheavals in which Ladakh found itself at different times. The force and agitation of an invading army is effectively depicted in **The Invader** (page 73). The detail here tells a tale of bloodshed, of fights between warring armies, of ephemeral hegemonies. It epitomises the rise and fall of many kingdoms and empires, violence and destruction, ferocity and massacres, to which Ladakh was subjected through the centuries. In contrast, on the same garment are also other scenes of a religious nature—shrines, holy men, fabulous flying Apsarases and Gandharvas—designed to inspire ineffable faith and hope in the devotee's supreme aspiration for peace. Stylistically, these paintings are an offshoot of Moghul miniature painting which, though transplanted and nourished in India, had its roots in Persia. Humayun, Babur's son, had lived in exile at the court of Shah Tahmasp, the Safavi ruler of Persia, where he became interested in manuscript painting. When he returned to India and recovered his throne in 1555 AD, Humayun brought with him from Kabul the painter, Sayyid Ali, and perphaps later his famous artist father, Mir Musavvir. Thus Persian miniatures in the Turkoman style (which had been centered on Shiraz, a city in southern Persia) gave new impetus to the already flourishing Indian schools, particularly at Malwa. An illustrated manuscript, the *Nimat Namah*, painted here thus became a source of inspiration to most schools of Indian miniatures.

In Ladakh, a variation of this style with strong intermingling of Khotanese mannerism seems to have developed during the time of Senge Namgyal who was himself a son of the Muslim wife of his predecessor, Jamwang Namgyal. The paintings covering the Bodhisattva's previously painted garments, described above, literally grafted a new theme in a new style onto Ladakh's ancient Buddhist traditions.

A VIEW OF THE RISONG MONASTERY, LADAKH.

Senge Namgyal's rule was the last spurt of the flame, as far as the art of the wall-paintings and sculpture of Ladakh was concerned. Soon after his death (1645 AD), the new Ladakhi style based on Moghul mannerism and inspired in the courts of the great Indian emperors, Akbar and Shahjehan, also ended with the accession of Aurangzeb in 1658 AD. The puritan Moghul emperor, Aurangzeb, had prohibited any form of visual art in his empire and these laws also became effective in Ladakh, when in 1664 AD Deden Namgyal accepted Aurangzeb's imperial decree to conform to his orthodox ideas. In these circumstances, the Buddhist art of wall-painting and large sculpture rapidly declined. More attention now began to be given to painting on cloth under conditions almost identical to those in Gujarat after the Muslim conquest at the end of the 13th Century AD. Like the Jain merchant community controlling trade and banking in western India, a new class of prosperous lama traders, flourishing on the Jisa system of decentralised treasuries, commissioned small objects of art which could be secretly made and worshipped in private.

LAHAUL AND SPITI

There is hardly a Buddhist shrine in the Himalaya that does not contain an image of the sage Padmasambhava (750-800 AD). According to tradition, it was at Riwalsar in the Punjab Hills that the teacher, who came from Uddiyana (the Swat valley), gave a popular basis to the mystical elements of Tantric philosophy and iconography. He thus became a symbol of the spirit of the time, in an age when Buddhist and Hindu practices and art forms practically lost their separate identity.

From the 7th Century onward, the art of the Himalaya cannot be seen in proper perspective without knowing what was happening in Tibet. Here, a dynastic line, whose influence prior to the period was localised in a small area south of the river Brahmaputra (Tsangpo), began to expand. The most outstanding of its kings, Srongtsen-gampo (died 650 AD), was converted to Buddhism by his minister, the famous Thonmi Sambhota, on his return from the Nalanda monastery in India after a course of study. Sambhota is also credited with having remodelled the Tibetan language on a basis of Sanskrit grammar. The next great protector of the faith was Trhisong-detsen, who came to the throne in 755 AD, and during whose reign the Vajrayana faith was introduced through the efforts of the legendary Padmasambhava, who was assisted in his missionary work by two eminent scholars from Nalanda, Santarakshita and his pupil, Tamalashila. Together they instituted Vajrayana, or what is popularly called the lamaist system, in Tibet and established the first Buddhist monastery at Samye. A vast literature developed around the story of Padmasambhava as well as prolific representations in sculpture and painting of his wonder-working conversions of devils and spirits of the native Bon cults. The fantastic stories of Padmasambhava's incredible powers found a responsive audience among the Tibetan artists and scholars. The great debate in the Buddhist Council of Lhasa (794 AD), at which the Chinese interpretation of the religion was rejected in favour of that propagated by Sri Ghosha and his companion, Kamalashila, further consolidated the Indian literary and art forms. After the death of Trhisong-detsen in 804, the third important king to advance this trend in Tibet was Ralpa-cen, who, on account of his religious merit, with his predecessors Srongtsen-gampo and Trhisong-detsen, became the representative on earth of the three family protectors—Vajrapani, Avalokiteshvara and Manjushri in that order; these deities are repeatedly depicted in hundreds of monasteries in the Himalaya. Ralpa-cen was a devout Buddhist and an uncompromising conformist who prohibited any activity which did not follow the accepted Indian type in Buddhist art or literature.

Padmasambhava is said to have travelled several times from Tibet to Kashmir via Riwalsar, despite the difficult journey involving three or four months. At the end of the 8th Century, he procured several Buddhist texts and craftsmen from Kashmir for the benefit of the

Samye monastery. In all, according to his biographer, his chief Tibetan disciple Yeshay-Chhogyal, Padmasambhava spent five years "travelling in the west".

Although Padmasambhava's specific routes of travel are not known, the tracks through the Himalaya had been well recognised since the time of Thonmi Sambhota, when he journeyed to Kashmir to learn the Sanskrit alphabet. The holiest of all mountains, Kailasha, by the sacred lake Manasarovara, could be approached from the important Buddhist country Jalandhara by following the river Sutlej upstream. This great river, with its source beyond the Indian frontiers, rises near the Dharma pass on the Zanskar range, and joining another tributary (the Langch-hen Khabab coming from the east through the Manasarovara and Rakas lakes) flows for about 250 kilometers through the Ngari Khorsum plateau of Tibet. It enters India at the Shipki pass in a south-westerly direction, cutting deep gorges through the Greater Himalaya, and then flows for nearly 300 kilometers before descending to the plains at Rupar. Guge was the name of the upper Sutlej valley which, as already mentioned, became a chief centre of Buddhist learning during saint Atisha's time; it was then that Rinchensangpo thrice travelled to Kashmir in search of Kashmiri craftsmen, probably along the tracks earlier traversed by Buddhist pilgrims. These were either the route down the Sutlej valley to India and then across the Siwalik range to the Beas valley and so to Kashmir, or the way through the Spiti and Chandra valleys to Ladakh and onward to the Kashmir valley. The routes apparently favoured by the Buddhist pilgrims were those to the south, leading to Jalandhara, Kullu and Kashmir.

In any case, these were—and still are—formidable footpaths winding their way through high snowy passes of great beauty and grandeur, and equally great hardship. The Inner Himalaya or Zanskar range at its eastern extremity separates Ladakh from Lahaul and Spiti and extends to the west forming the northern boundary of Kashmir. The passes through this spectacular barrier of granite covered with permanent glaciers are over 5,180 meters high. Towards the north is another towering range called Baralacha from which rise two rivers, the Bhaga and Chandra, which enclose the Lahaul valley. The rivers unite at a place called Thand to become the river Chenab, which then flows alongside the Pangi range to the north of the town of Chamba. Towards the east is the source of the river Beas at the Rohtang pass (4,100 meters) and beyond this near the river Chandra is the Kunzum pass (4,500 meters), where the river Spiti is born. The Spiti winds through a desolate landscape, a wild waste of stones and shale at an average height of 3,300 meters, to join the Sutlej. The northern area, called the "Tsarab", adjoins the Lingti plain of Lahaul and its waters drain off through it to the river Indus.

In this bleak atmosphere of raw and rugged nature, of awe-inspiring high peaks and swift torrents, from the fears of the travellers naturally emerged deities such as the Lords of Soil (Sabdag). These were more than mountain gods on whose mercy and protection depended human survival. At first they were represented merely by an upright stick in the centre of a round base of stones and pebbles. This symbol is the simplest form of the Lingam (phallus), the most common basic object of Shiva worship. This form can be traced back to the worship of primitive stone symbols as early as the 3rd millennium BC at Mohenjodaro. At this ancient site the Lingam was depicted beside other figures similar to those later seen in Indian art. Lingam, the male creative energy of Shiva in contradistinction to other potentialities of this god, is called Dhruva or "fixed or immovable". It is also Mulavigraha or "the fundamental form". For the people living in the Himalaya there is nothing more "fixed or immovable" than the gigantic mountains and hence the Lingam became their most appropriate symbol. During the Gupta period, Shiva was already represented as Mukhalinga or a male member with a god's head, like a Greek *herma*. In the Himalaya Shiva's trident was also borrowed and it was placed over an ornamental skull. These symbols also represent the mountain peaks, Kye-phang of Lahaul, Jam-la of Spiti and Purgyal of Kunawar. Another name for Sabdag is Thug, and the symbols are repeatedly erected by Vajrayana followers on the top of the Buddhist shrines. **A Lord of Soil** (page 111) is one such fantastic symbol which is placed over the famous monastery of Kye in Spiti. The flaming Trisula (trident) in gold placed over a marvellous silver sculpture of a skull is a production of great skill and imagination. It makes an unforgettable impression against the backdrop of the clear, glowing sky and the graded browns of the high mountains.

The sentinel-like cones of the mountain summits produce a phantasy of huge monsters staring down from the dizzy heights. At dawn, when the rays of the rising sun fall upon the frozen, muscular masks of these giants, they appear to awake with weird contortions on their faces; their colours and expressions alter as they seem to move slowly in a dancing rhythm, changing with the position of the sun. It is, therefore, no wonder that the primitive inhabitants of the Himalaya also spontaneously translated their surroundings into the shapes of an incredible variety of masks. **A Wooden Mask** (page 103) is a fantastic piece of workmanship, simple yet effective. It is a reflection of the spirits and devils of Bon-po beliefs about magic, sorcery and superstition. On gay festive occasions and at times of ill fortune, these replicas of mountain images are worn by traditional dancers who invariably appear on the scene to assist the occasion with their slow rhythm, in time to deep-sounding drums echoing in the valleys. The Bon-po cult has long been superseded by the Buddhist religion, but these basic art forms of an ageless variety are firmly enshrined in the mental make-up and religious and artistic responses of the hardy, truthful and kind-hearted people of Lahaul and Spiti.

A WOODEN MASK, GURUGHANTAL MONASTERY,
LAHAUL VALLEY. 16th—17th CENTURY AD.

As early as 327-26 BC, when Alexander the Great invaded the Punjab,
be met with a number of small principalities, which later united under
the gigantic empire of the Mauryas, whose famous emperor Ashoka was
converted to Buddhism and spread its message with a missionary zeal.
The western Himalaya also came under Ashoka's sway in the 3rd Century BC, as indicated by his rock edicts at Kalsi. Another inscription
in mixed Brahmi and Khoroshti script (200 BC) at Kanhiara and

103

Pathyar also speaks of the foundation of a Buddhist monastery there. The disintegration of Ashoka's empire about 185 BC does not seem to have disturbed the Buddhist hold in the western Himalaya as, after an interlude of invasions by the Bactrian Greeks, the Indo-Parthians and the Indo-Scythians, the religion flourished in the Siwalik when it became a part of the Kushan empire (c. 50 BC-210 AD).

During this period, the principal ethnic settlers here seem to have been the Khashas, who spread over Kashgar in Central Asia, Kashmir, Nepal and even Assam, while the Kunindas and Audumbaras inhabited the valleys of the Ravi, Beas and Sutlej. Later, some of the Kunindas appear to have migrated to Kumaon, and on the banks of the Sutlej lived the Vrishnis, on the Beas the Audumbaras and Kapisthalas, on the Ravi the Kathas and Darvas and in the valleys of the Chenab the Rajanyas. All these tribes were vassals of the Kushans, under whose rule the Buddhist art of the plains had already begun infiltrating the hills, as can be seen from the ruins of a Stupa at Chetru, near Kangra, and some very interesting images from the coins of the Audumbaras (c. 2nd-3rd Centuries AD).

Subsequently, when Kushan authority was shaken by the Bharashivas of Bundelkhand (who re-establised a semi-imperial authority in north India), the Hindu influence gradually increased. The Bharashiva Naga kings were the followers of Shiva and significantly described themselves as those "who secured the favour of Shiva by carrying his trident on their shoulders". The relentless advance of the Barashivas against the then receding power of the Kushans seems to have necessitated the establishment of branch families at centres such as Bidisa and Mathura. According to some authors, at this time quite a few "Rajput" warriors seem to have secured a foothold in the Punjab Hills. The newcomers are said to have been the followers of a Pashupata ascetic Lakulisha (born c. 125 AD) in Gujarat, who was the author of the *Pashupata Sutras* and the sect called Lakulpashupata took root in this region with the establishment of important centres at Maruta Math, Udaipur in Chamba-Lahaul and Gurughantal, above the junction of the rivers Bhaga and Chandra in the Lahaul valley.

With the ascendancy of the imperial Guptas, Samudragupta (328-76 AD) and his famous successor Chandragupta II Vikramaditya (378-414 AD) conquered vast areas in the Himalaya.

From the excellent late Gupta sculptures found at Agroha near Hissar (now in the Chandigarh East Punjab museum), Kapalmochan and Pinjaur, it is evident that the Gupta style then popular in the empire of the great Harshavardhana of Thanesar (606-64 AD) had also penetrated the territories and vassal kingdoms in the valleys of the Ravi, Beas and Sutlej. Out-of-the-way areas such as Lahaul and Spiti also apparently came under its sway as, according to the tradition observed at the Triloknath shrine, Harshavardhana inaugurated the "unification" of Hinduism and Buddhism. At the great asemblies witnessed by the

104

A COUPLE WARMING THEIR HANDS OVER A STOVE.

Chinese Buddhist pilgrim, Hsuan Tsang, Harshavardhana had installed "images of the Buddha, Adityadeva (the sun) and Ishvaradeva (Shiva) on successive days". Vajrayana Buddhism transformed many Hindu deites and incorporated them into its Mandalas, and these analogies greatly increased when the Buddhist deities abandoned human form by multiplying their heads and arms. Halahalavalokiteshvara· and Nilakanthaavalokiteshvara are remarkable derivatives of Shiva, while Brahma influenced the popular Buddhist deity Manjushri; also when Manjushri is assigned Karttikeya's vehicle, the peacock, as his symbol he is called Manjushrikarttikeya. The Buddhists, in fact, absorbed all kinds of attractive Hindu tenets, ideas, dogmas, theories, rites and practices, for which they created images projecting the deep-rooted mythological symbols which were near and dear to the popular imagination.

Among the oldest surviving shrines in the Lahaul valley where joint Hindu-Buddhist worship was conducted in the 8th Century AD is said to be Gurughantal. In this temple there is a sculpture of a marble head, which was dug up in the valley below the junction of the rivers

Chandra and Bhaga. **Avalokiteshvara** (page 116) is said to have been consecrated by Padmasambhava himself which is quite possible considering its age. The plastic austerity and stylistic sophistication of this exquisite piece, with hypnotising eyes under gently arched eyebrows, have all the qualities of Gupta classicism. This figure is by far the finest of all the stray Gupta sculptures of the 7th-8th Centuries traced at Kullu, Kangra, Chamba and Asarur. The silky softness and warmth of the flesh and the slightly smiling dignified expression are achieved by the marvellously rounded face and the mildly upturned corners of the lips. The crown is typically Gupta-Kashmiri in construction with elaborate designs of jewels and strings of beads which gracefully dangle in semi-circles from equidistant points of support in the hair. The roundel in the crown above the forehead in which the Dhyani-buddha is chiselled has unfortunately been damaged; but as the head, according to tradition, is of Bodhisattva Avalokiteshvara, the figure in the roundel is undoubtedly the Dhyani-buddha Amitabha. The vogue of making sculptures in marble had become common during the age of Harshavardhana of Thanesar, when marble from Rajasthan and also as far away as the Vindhyas was used for this purpose.

The stylistic history of art summed up in this lovely head not only contains the mysteries of the events of the chaotic years following Harshavardhana's death, but also the marvellous renaissance in art which was ushered in by patrons such as Meruvarman of Brahmor and Lalitaditya of Kashmir. Lahaul was occupied by Brahmor in about 600 AD and later by the Karkota dynast. The sculpture also hints at the interaction of these styles with those of Kanauj which became marked after 730 AD, when the Kashmiri monarch defeated Yashovarman and the latter became Lalitaditya's viceroy.

The original temple of Sandhya Devi at the village of Jagatsukh, near Kullu, which is stylistically associated with the Kanauj of Ayudhya dynasty, shows that the mixed Gupta-Kashmiri style was further enriched by influences percolating from that dynasty under the suzerainty of the Pala kingdom of Bengal and Bihar, as a result of advances deep into the western Himalaya by Dharmapala (*c.* 770-815 AD) and Devapala (*c.* 815-54 AD). Several bronzes in the Pala style at Chatrarhi in Chamba, at Kullu and in the Lahaul and Spiti valleys indicate that from the 8th Century Siwalik's cultural contacts with Bengal and Bihar were almost continuous. The Pala art prototype were apparently brought by the refugees fleeing from the plains and by pilgrims, especially after Padmasambhava's name became a legend after the 9th Century AD. Apart from Riwalsar, which is a sacred place of pilgrimage for the Hindus and the Buddhists alike, Padmasambhava's name is associated with Nako in the lower Spiti valley (Kunawar), where there is a small ancient temple built on his supposed footprints on rock. **Bodhisattva Manjushri** (page 113) which is said to have been cast in this area is clearly a bronze of Pala inspiration. But by this time

AVALOKITESHVARA, TABO MONASTERY, SPITI VELLEY. 15th CENTURY AD.

the avalanche of Tantric philosophy had already overwhelmed the best
in the "Kadam" style in image casting. This can be seen particularly
from the style of the crown which is more like the form very popular
in Guge during Atisha's time. The earlier simpler tenets are here replaced by some of the more occult concepts, such as the bejewelled
Buddha as an emblem of the resplendent body. The bronzes from the
Pala kingdom supplied the models for the later Buddhist art in Tibet
and Nepal and the differences between the originals and the ones

107

that were transplanted are mainly confined to such surface elaborations as stylised lotus flowers, crowns and the thrones on which the deities are seated.

Images of Manjushri are not found in the Gandhara and Mathura schools of sculpture, but in the later period, especially in the Himalaya, Manjushri's place in the Buddhist pantheon is one of the very highest. It was believed that the worship of Manjushri could confer wisdom, retentive memory, intelligence and eloquence for the mastery of sacred scriptures. Almost every Buddhist shrine in the Himalaya has an image of this deity. He is conceived in various forms, of which the simplest is the one in which he carries the sword in his right hand and the *Prajnaparamita* manuscript in his left. Sometimes, as in this case, the manuscript is represented by a lotus flower. There are at least 41 forms in the *Sadhanamala* which are devoted to the worship of Manjushri and in which several distinct forms of the Bodhisattva are described.

The various stylistic influences penetrating Lahaul and its neighbouring territories continued unabated during the 10th and 11th Centuries AD. They were carried on the waves of advancing and waning fortunes of the kingdoms trying to control these areas. After Toramana (903-40 AD) and Bhimapala (*c*. 940-65 AD), who had tried to annex territories beyond the Ravi, the Shahis with their relations with Kashmir succeeded in expanding their influence over the eastern Punjab, the Kangra valley and Lahaul and Spiti under Jayapala (965-1001 AD). On the other hand, with the decline of the Pratihara empire, one of the military governors of the western Pratihara frontier, Shahilavarman (c. 920-40 AD), established himself in Trigarta and consolidated his power into a semi-independent kingdom with its capital at Chambra. During his reign and later under the patronage of his successor, Yugakaravarman (940-60 AD), were built some of the most monumental and magnificent temples, west of the Sutlej. After 964 AD, the authority of Chamba progressively weakened until it was invaded by king Anantadeva of Kashmir (1028-63 AD) and Raja Salavahana was defeated and killed in 1060 AD. Later, this area changed hands, once again, when king Lhachen Utpala of Ladakh (*c*. 1080-1110 AD) invaded and conquered Kullu and also wrested the control of Lahaul from king Kalasha of Kashmir (*c*. 1063-89 AD). These see-saw political battles were paralleled in styles, so that during this period two distinct groups of styles seem to have alternated according to which ruler was in power. The group from the west was dominated by sophisticated, slim Kashmiri elegance, while the other was led by Pratihara mannerism created during the period when its emperors had become merely puppets in the hands of the Chandellas. In contrast to the Kashmiri style, Chandella art believed in plump figures, sensuous and sexy curves, as seen in the grossly erotic sculptures made under its patronage at Khajuraho (954-1002 AD). During this process of changing political fortunes as well as art pa-

tronage, several elements of style belonging to these two groups were also exchanged. But by this time the two major styles had crystallised to such an extent that they maintained their basic forms.

Marichi Vajravarahi (page 115) is a beautiful example of an elegant Kashmiri model. This magnificent sculpture in clay, studded with precious stones, gold and silver, is in the monastery of Gemur in the Lahaul valley. Its lovely elongated round limbs, shapely breast and elegant and sophisticated posture are reminiscent of several sculptures and paintings at the Alchi and Tabo shrines. The popularity and the diffusion of this style are evident from the entrance of the Nam-par-snag-mdzad temple at Alchi which has several stylistic resemblances also with the door jambs and niches of the facade of the Markula shrine. Two beautifully carved panels in the Tabo monastery in Spiti have almost exact replicas of similar Kashmiri niches, said to have been put up at Rinchen-sangpo's command. Also, the elegant and slim figures depicted in the carvings of these temples have remarkable analogies with the painted clay figures of the Buddha accompanied by Vajrapani and Avalokiteshvara in the temple at Tsaparang (Guge). This period coincides with the reign of Anantadeva of Kashmir (1028-63 AD), who soon after the death of queen Didda (1063 AD) restored Kashmir's control over the Punjab hill states. During his invasion of Chamba, Anantadeva overthrew and killed the Chamba sovereign, Salavahana, thus establishing his suzerainty over Chamba, Kashtwar and Lahaul. The name Vajravarahi or "adamantine sow" is given to this goddess due to the excrescence resembling a sow near her right ear. The Tantric Buddhist text *Sadhanamala* describes the goddess thus: "The worshipper should think himself as goddess Vajaravarahi, whose colour is red like the pomegranate flower and has two arms. She exhibits in her right hand the Vajra along with the raised index finger, and shows in the left the Kapala and the Khatvanga. She has one face, three eyes, dishevelled hair and stands naked marked with six auspicious symbols. She is the essence of five kinds of knowledge and is the embodiment of the Sahaje pleasure. She stands in the Pratyalidha attitude, tramples upon the gods Bhairava and Kalaratri, and wears a garland of heads still wet with blood which she drinks".

In contrast with this style is the fantastic figure of **A Pancharaksha Goddess** (page 114), depicted in a mural in the Tayul monastery near Keylong. Chief of the Pancha Rakshas (five protectors), according to Foucher, is Maha-Sahasrapramardini, who is the deification of a spell to ward off earthquakes and storms. The other goddesses are Mahamantranusarini to the east protecting the world from all disease; Mahapratisara to the south averting evil forces and physical dangers; Mahasitavati guarding against ferocious animals and evil plants; and Mahamayuri representing spells against snake bites. The image reproduced here does not strictly follow all the iconographical attributes assigned to any one of the goddesses. As often happened in this late

A LORD OF SOIL, KYE MONASTERY, SPITI VALLEY. 16th CENTURY AD.

period of diminishing knowledge of iconometry, the painters of this image have mixed up the various symbols for each of the five goddesses into a fantastic conception.

The Pancha Raksha goddess is here depicted with nine heads, each with three eyes, in addition to the eyes all over the upper part of her body. She is seen emerging from the cosmic ocean with terrific force, holding a bow and an arrow in her left hand and a dragon-headed serpent in her right. The curling, slithering goddess, the lower half of whose body is in the shape of a snake, appears to add to the agitation of the whirlpool, thus producing a fearful storm.

The figure is interesting because of the several eyes with which her body is covered. The third eye in the forehead is a later development in Buddhist iconography, and at some stage the Dhyani-buddha Amogh-asiddhi was assigned this additional attribute. The earliest Budhhist deities were apparently depicted with additional eyes on the backs of their hands, in conformity with the convention which started with the Bhumisparsamudra or "the earth touching gesture" of the Buddha's hands when he attained enlightenment. There are very few surviving examples of painting showing the solitary third eye on the back of the hand in the Himalayan monasteries; but the tradition seems to have been preserved in Central Asia, as shown by a remarkable early 7th Century wall painting from Balawaste, now preserved at the National Museum in New Delhi. In the Himalaya, the extension of this idea, by which the eyes were infinitely multiplied, became popular by the 15th Century AD.

The Pancharaksha goddesses are the Buddhist version of one of the most popular legends of Indian mythology, which is told with numerous variations in the *Ramayana, Mahabharata* and *Puranas*. According to this myth, Amrita (the nectar of immortality) was produced when the gods, having been worsted by the demons, approached Vishnu for help and he directed them to churn the cosmic ocean to obtain it. Vishnu, called Ananta-shayin, "he who sleeps on the serpent Ananta", was also symbolised by the Buddhists who, in keeping with the Tantric emphasis, identified him with these goddesses and also Rahaul. The goddess being half-human and half-serpent is the dual manifestation of humanity as well as the ocean since, according to mythology, the serpent is the symbol of water. The cosmos is graphically depicted as a face on her belly symbolising an unborn babe of primal perfection, whose mother, the goddess, is both in an anthropomorphic shape and in the form of the element water, which has no horizon. Thus, she represents the apparition of all life emerging out of formless primal substance, water, illustrating the mirage-like character of all phenomenal earthly and divine existence.

Unlike the painters of the high Kashmiri style who took delight in slim shapely figures, the artist here is more concerned with the pervading effects of light and the gradation of colour, and has interpreted the

BODDHISATTVA MANJUSHRI, NAKO MONASTERY, SPITI VALLEY.
10th—11th CENTURY AD.

A PANCHARAKSHA GODDESS, TAYUL MONASTERY, LAHAUL VALLEY.
16th CENTURY AD.

AVALOKITESHVARA, GURUGHANTAL MONASTERY, LAHAUL VALLEY, 8th CENTURY AD.

MARICHI VAJRAVAHARI, GEMUR MONASTERY, LAHAUL VALLEY.
11th—12th CENTURY AD.

figure in a style seen in Chandella sculptures. This style, while retaining the hard vigour and violence of the 8th Century is, nevertheless, enriched by the continuous influence from Kashmir, by local folk art and hints from the Rajput court traditions. In fact, it is an admixture of the voluptuous sexy figures of the heavy rustic Trigarta style which inspired similar art at some of the sculptures in Jagatsukh, near Kullu.

Among the earliest Buddhist divinities depicted with several heads, arms and eyes is **Avalokiteshvara** (page 107). The one head and two arms of this ancient image (in the form called Padmapani) were multiplied during the Tantric period, so that the wondrous figure became Chentong Chhaktong with a thousand eyes and a thousand arms. The motif of covering the body with numerous eyes is also clearly derived from the *Mahabharata* version of a legend attributed to Indra. When Indra endeavoured to seduce Ahalya, the wife of sage Gautama, the sage's curse impressed upon him a thousand marks resembling the female organ. However, Sa-Yoni, as Indra was now called, with his spiritual powers changed these marks into eyes, so that Indra became Sahasrasha (the thousand-eyed). As in this figure in the famous Tabo monastery in the lower Spiti valley, the arms like spokes of a wheel are contained in the shape of a scallop shell, while an open eye on the palm of every hand represents the inexhaustible mystery of the divine. Avalokiteshvara can also be represented with five heads, like Shiva as Mahadeva, and in this form he holds his Shakti on his knee in the archaic manner. His Yab-Yum form in which he holds his female counterpart in an embrace is also known.

After the conquest of western Lahaul by Raja Pratap Singh of Chamba (1557-82 AD), several of the Buddhist temples were once again reconverted to their earlier Hindu allegiance, so that the Buddhist goddess Vajravarahi was replaced by Kali. However, for the common people this does not seem to have made much difference as, in keeping with the tradition inaugurated by Padmasambhava, both the goddesses were considered to be merely different manifestations of the Great Goddess.

THE SIWALIK RANGES

SHULAPANI-SHIVA AND PARVATI, STANDING WITH NANDI, CHAMBA.
5th CENTURY AD.

The outer ranges of the Himalaya between the valleys of the rivers Chanab and Sutlej are commonly called the Siwalik even though this name is broadly applicable to the entire area of the Himalayan foothills. These consist of a series of parallel ridges and valleys rising to a maximum height of about 1,500 meters. Between the Chanab and the Ravi rivers is the region of Dugar (Jammu), which comprises the tiny

SHULAPANI-SHIVA AND PARVATI, SITTING ON NANDI, CHATRARHL. 8th—9th CENTURY AD.

VISHNU AND LAKSHMI, CHAMBA. 10th CENTURY AD.

states of Basohli, Jasrota and Mankot. Further east, between the Ravi and the Sutlej, are the small states of Kangra, Guler, Chamba, Mandi, Nurpur and Kullu. Formerly, this area was known as Trigarta and included the unsurpassable grandeur and loveliness of the river valleys of the Ravi, Beas and Sutlej. The Pir Panjal range of Kashmir, with its snow-covered summits rising to over 5,000 meters, enters Himachal Pradesh north of the headwaters of the Ravi and runs eastwards, forming the watershed between the river Chanab in the north and the Ravi and Beas rivers in the south. The Chamba state lies next to Kashmir, the southern banks of the river Ravi forming the boundary between lower Jammu and Chamba state. To the south of the river and almost parallel to it is the Dhaula Dhar range which runs towards the Beas valley in a great curve with its convex side facing the Kangra valley. The upper Beas flows through the beautiful valley of Kullu flanked by the magnificent peaks Deo Tibba (6.001 meters) and Indrasan (6,220 meters). This valley is connected through the Rohtang pass to the valleys of Lahaul and Spiti over the Pangi range which to the north-west enters and traverses the Chamba territory. The eastern Siwalik ranges of the Simla Hill States mainly follow the Sutlej river and here are situated Bilaspur and, beyond Simla near the source of the river Ganges, Tehri-Garhwal.

The *Vamshavalis* or genealogical rolls of the rulers, the few coins and other scattered information revealed by inscriptions do not give a reliable history of the early centuries after Christ. It is fairly certain, however, that in the Siwalik the migration of refugees continued as they were driven to the hills before the tide of barbarian invaders who were overrunning the Gupta empire. Among these newcomers were the groups from the hordes of Drugga barbarians who were the first to attack the Gupta empire. These elements appear to have settled in Marwar and southern Gujarat where their influence can be seen in the art of Idar (early 6th Century AD), the Jain bronzes from Vasantgarh and Akotta (*c.* 7th Century AD) and a few other stone sculptures of the 7th-8th Centuries AD from Jaisalmer and Kiradu. They later joined hands with the White Huns and seem finally to have settled in Rajasthan and Gujarat. There is a theory that these people, broadly called the Gur-jaras, some of whom also migrated to the hills and called themselves Rajputs, were partly responsible for the introduction of the later Gupta art forms in the region.

This is a theory and whether or not the Gurjara actually established a state in the Siwalik in the 6th Century AD is controversial. It is, however, certain that the assortment of immigrants who made their homes in the foothills of the Himalaya at this time became more and more Hinduised. By the 8th Century AD these people, like the original in-habitants, seem to have become devotees of Shiva. The *Padma-thangyig*, which is attributed to Padmasambhava, contains a reference to Maruta Mat in the Punjab Hills as one of the ancient sacred places of worship by Shiva's followers.

Most of the early monuments in the Himalaya were made of wood and other perishable material and have consequently disappeared, leav-ing us no examples of art belonging to the early centuries after Christ. Vague hints are provided by such relics as the coins of the Audumbaras (2nd-3rd Centuries AD), which depict railings resembling those which were erected around the early Buddhist Stupas. But on these coins the railings enclose Chaityavrikshas (sacred trees) and hut-like shrines. Fertility symbols, such as images of female goddesses, and snakes, like those still occurring in Himalayan folk art, are also seen on these relics. Siwalik's heritage of the imperial Gupta art tradition can only be deduced from the transition in style from the cube-like early Gupta shrines to the medieval temple towers. There is also evidence to show

PEASANTS PLOUGHING AND SOWING.

that Gupta art gained a strong foothold in the hills for the first time in the 6th-8th Centuries AD, first under Ashodharman, then under the Maukharis and Pushyabhutis. In Chaunsa Bawar (Kumaon), Gupta sculptures have been found in a Shiva temple which was erected by a princess Ishvara of Singhapura (600 AD). Singhapura is also referred to by the Chinese pilgrim Hsuan Tsant as Song-ho-pu-lo, which was a vassal kingdom of Kashmir, probably to the north of the Salt Range. Among the sculptures at Chaunsa Bawar, there is a fine group with Shiva and Parvati, the most popular deities of this period. **Shulapani-Shiva and Parvati standing with Nandi** (page 120) is another important piece which, like the already well-known Surya image from Gum, was found in the Ravi valley, halfway between Chamba and Brahmor.

This piece, showing figures standing on a Gupta plinth or platform and chiselled in the Gupta style, also reflects strong Kashmiri influences. Like the Surya image, the sculpture may belong to the earlier period when Maukhari-Gupta influence had not completely overwhelmed the Sassano-Kushan art of Gandhara. Moreover, the standing bull, behind the deity, also represents a survival of an earlier iconographical practice peculiar to the mountains of north-western India. Shiva with a trident in one of his hands (Shulapani) in a standing posture in front of an upright bull is known from several Kushan, Kidara-Kushan and Kushano-Sassanian coins. This style therefore very probably reflects the original influences from Kashmir where, after the withdrawal of the Huns, there appears to have occurred a revival of the cult forms in vogue during the Kushan period. The reverse side of this stone bas-relief is also typical of the style seen in some of the sculptures of Gandhara, even though the barrel-shaped body of the animal very much resembles the shape of the bull Nandi in the Lakshana Devi temple, preserved in king Meruvarman's capital at Brahmor.

Unfortunately, Meruvarman's reign has been dated by paleographical evidence only and scholars differ on the subject. While some experts have placed him in the middle of the 7th Century AD, others prefer the end of the century. There are still those who consider him to be roughly contemporary with the Kashmiri monarch Lalitaditya Mukta-pida (c. 725-56 AD) and in some kind of a subordinate alliance with him. On stylistic grounds alone, the latter view appears to be more plausible. In this period, Kashmir and the Siwalik regions were in close cultural contact as is shown by the architectural designs of temples such as the Manimahesha, Lakshana Devi, Narsimha and Ganesha temples at Brahmor and also by some of the most exquisite of the well-known bronzes such as the images of Lakshana Devi at Brahmor and Shakti Devi at Chatarhi.

Recently, a few smaller pieces have come to light which show the absorption of the Meruvarman style into the Kashmiri sphere of influence. One example is **Shulapani-Shiva and Parvati sitting on Nandi** (page 121). Apart from its great age, this piece is especially interesting both iconographically and stylistically in comparison with Shulapani-Shiva and Parvati standing with Nandi (page 125). The plinth as well as the general conception of the bronze piece is still distinctly Gupta in style, but the bull Nandi is now conventionally lying down, in a relaxed position with all four legs drawn in. The symbols represented by smaller deities are on the platform, but reduced in number, so that one displaced deity is now seated on the ground beside the plinth. A striking feature is also the typcial Kashmiri-style modelling of the combined halo and Vesica, but the flames marked with wavy lines as seen in Kashmir bronzes do not yet make their appearance. The slim, elegant bodies covered with almost transparent clothes, the high diadem decorated with two jewelled flowers above each ear, from which scarves flow

NATIVE MILKMEN AND IRONSMITHS.

down on the shoulders, resemble the manner of casting seen in the
famous image of Shakti Devi in the Chatrarhi temple. Chatrarhi is a
village situated in a fertile upland on the slope south of the Ravi, not
far from Chamba. Its foundation is attributed to Mushana, the legendary
ancestor of the old Brahmor dynasty, but the inscription on the Shakti
Devi image mentions Meruvarman, the founder of Brahmor. The tradition also has it that it was the last work of Gugga, the master artisan
of Meruvarman. However, the iconographical similarity between Shulapani Shiva and Parvati sitting on Nandi and the image of Shakti Devi
ends with the garment which covers the upper part of Parvati's body.
This appears to be made up of two pieces sewn on the upper part
while the lower part of the "blouse" has pointed corners revealing
partings above the hips.
The Brahmaputa kingdom formed an important link between Gupta art
forms and the expansion of Hindu civilisation. The Gupta civilisation,

KRISHNA LILA. RANG MAHAL PALACE, CHAMBA. LATE 18th CENTURY AD.

though mortally wounded by the Hun attacks, for several centuries resisted the barbarian invasions and at the same time absorbed the culture of the nomadic hordes into its framework. In this process, beginning in the 6th Century AD, the kingdoms of Broach, Bhinmal and Mandor as well as Brahmapura had adopted the best achievements of both the late Gupta and the medieval Hindu civilisation by the 8th Century AD. Apparently, the various influences of the preceding period were brought together in a hybrid style which was perhaps created by the artist Shringadhara, to whom Taranatha referred in his *History of Buddhism.* According to the Tibetan historian, "The skilful delineator of gods was born in Marwar and left behind paintings and other masterpieces, which resemble those produced by the Yakshas". Shringadhara is associated by Taranatha with "King Shila" and possibly he was either an artist at the court of Harshavardhana (606-64 AD) or of his famous father, Prabhakaravardhana; the latter was the son of a princess of "later Gupta lineage". These rulers had their capital in Thanesar in the Punjab, not far from the foothills of the Himalaya. Shringadhara's models apparently inspired the exquisite art pieces created by the artisan Gugga. Then, from the Punjab Hills, these art forms penetrated into Kashmir, as is evident from Taranatha's description which also, chronologically, has placed "Hasuraja's Kashmiri school" at a later period. Nevertheless, due to the predominance of the political power exercised by the Karkota empire, the Siwalik ranges in the 8th Century AD became known within the sphere of influence of Kashmiri art. At Mandi there are vestiges of carvings in the Kashmiri style in a fortress guarding the Rohtang pass, and two carved wooden reliefs in the same style and period stand at Maylang in Lahaul. In Chamba-Lahaul, also, vestiges of Kashmiri art can be traced at Triloknath and at Markula-Udaipur. In fact, the Kashimiri circle of influence encompassed a large area including Brahmor, where the top gable of the Lakshana Devi temple and the marble head of The Bodhisattva are evidence of this.

Cultural influences from central and eastern India had already begun to take root in the Siwalik ranges and Kashmir when Yashovarman accepted the supremacy of Lalitaditya of Kashmir and became his viceroy at Kanauj. We also know from the *Rajatrangini* that, after his victory over Kanauj in 733 AD, Lalitaditya had sent political opponents and hostages back to Kashmir during his campaigns further east. Among his hostages was Jivitagupta, the last ruler of the later dynasty of imperial Guptas in Magadha (Bihar and Bengal). Artistic exchanges with eastern India brought about by these events were maintained even after the disintegration of the Karkota empire when in about 770 AD the Ayudhya kings superseded the last weak successors of Yashovarman; but they, in turn, came to be dominated by the power of the Palas of Bengal. A number of Buddhist bronzes, found both in Kullu and Chatrarhi, are a pointer to the cultural interchange during the dependence of the Ayudhya kings of Kanauj on Dharmapala and Revapala

who reigned over the Bengal-Bihar Pala kingdom. According to tradition, a number of Buddhists from the famous Buddhist "universities" are said to have come on pilgrimages to Riwalsar, near Mandi, where in the second half of the 8th Century AD resided the great Tantric Buddhist sage, Padmasambhava.

The consolidation of the Pratihara empire after the conquest of Kanauj by Nagabhatta II, gave a jolt to the sophisticated elegance of art styles in the Himalaya, especially when his grandson Bhoja (*c.* 833-85 AD) came to power. Under this king, Adivaraha Mihira Bhoja I, the Pratihara empire consisted of all the provinces from central Bihar in the east to the river Ravi in the Punjab, from the Himalayan valleys in the north southwards to Gujarat, Saurashtra, Malwa and central India. Although the advance of this powerful ruler towards north-western India was checked by Shankaravarman of Kashmir, his reign saw the diffusion of a new, powerful and aggressive style throughout the Kanauj dependencies in the 9th Century AD. Terrible and majestic figures, with stiff expressions, ponderous looks and scant ornaments, were mainly depicted in the more demoniac manifestations of Shiva and his consort Parvati. Also popular were the sons of these deities, the elephant-headed Ganesha and powerful Karttikeya with his six heads. **Karttikeya** (page 131) in the small temple of Khaknal between Kullu and Mandi, is a product of this style, as interpreted in the hills. His massive, broad shoulders, the symmetrical archaic arches formed by his two principal hands and the inscrutable expressions on his six faces are here completely in harmony with the sturdy, rough conception of the peacock standing behind this god of war. The crude, rustic atmosphere created by the sculptor is, all the same, very charming. Karttikeya, also called Skanda, is considered to be the son of Shiva and to have been born without a female's intervention, even though Shiva's consort, Parvati, and Ganga (the river Ganges) are occasionally represented to be his mother. (As the legend has it, Shiva cast his seed into fire and it was received by Ganga.) Karttikeya is so called because he was fostered by Krittika, Pleiades, and has six heads. His vehicle is the peacock called Paravani and his consort is Kaumari or Sena. He is usually represented holding a bow in one hand an arrow in the other. Tantric images, as in this case, assigned him with more than two hands holding various symbols.

Karttikeya is a favourite god in the Himalaya because, it is said, he keeps open the passes in the mountains. The *Vayu Purana* credits him with splitting open with his arrow the Himalayan pass Krauncha to make a passage from Kailasha towards the south. Indra, the sky god, and Karttikeya had a dispute about their respective powers, to decide which they ran a race round the Himalaya. The finish was so close that they appealed to Himavat (Himalaya) who unjustly decided in Indra's favour. Karttikeya, in disappointed rage, hurled his lance at the mountains, piercing a pass through them.

VISHNU AND LAKSHMI ON GARUDA,
BILASPUR. 13th—14th AD.

KARTTIKEYA, KHAKNAL TEMPLE NEAR
KULLU. 9th—10th AD.

The Kashmiri style, evolved under Lalitaditya, then refined under the
patronage of Avantivarman and Shankaravarman, continued to be practised in the Siwalik region, west of the Ravi. By the middle of the
9th Century AD, after Bhoja's ambitions in the north-west had been
checked by the kingdom of Kashmir, a critical point seems to have
been reached also in art styles of the hills. The classical art of the
later Guptas, refined and polished in the sophisticated courts of Lalitaditya of Kashmir and Meruvarman of Brahmor, clashed with the rustic,
forthright and down-to-earth art style of Kanauj. The result, apparently,
was the development of two parallel styles which, in one form or other,
continued to be practised in succeeding centuries. Even in the 10th
Century AD when these areas at last developed into a pure Rajput
vassal state of the Pratiharas and the later Pratihara art forms became
more elegant, the early Pratihara art forms continued to be more or less
preserved in the hills. They owe their existence not so much to the

131

patronage of the rulers as to the loyalty of the common people; this style produced a sympathetic response in the folk art and cults practised by local tribes, such as the Gurjaras, Khashas, Gaddis, etc.

In stone, the clash between the two styles, Kashmiri and the rustic art forms of Kanauj, was more pronounced than in casting of bronzes. In the sphere of bronzes, there is evidence of a greater effort to absorb the new influences into already accepted art forms, as can be seen in some very remarkable pieces made under the patronage of Shahilavarman, who founded the city of Chamba (920 AD). One such example is **Vishnu and Lakshmi** (page 121). It shows Vishnu squatting in a peculiar position, unknown to the Kashmiri style, with the toes of his two feet almost touching each other, a typical posture still seen in India today. His vehicle Garuda is depicted in a miniature size, more to indicate the identity of the god than as part of the composition. The strength displayed by Vishnu's broad chest and shoulders, his majestic erect

MAHISHASURAMARDINI, BAJAURA TEMPLE, KULLU. LATE 10th CENTURY AD.

SHIVA ARDHANARI, ARDHANARI TEMPLE, MANDI. 16th CENTURY AD.

posture, the stern expression on his face are all a natural culmination of a trend which started in the 8th Century AD when Gupta art reached its last phase, connected with Yashovarman of Kanauj (c. 700-52 AD). The Gupta canon here is still more or less intact but, obviously due to early Pratihara influences, the sculpture has acquired a pompous vitality, verging on hardness and exaggerated mannerism.

With the decline of the Karkota dynasty in Kashmir, the early rulers of the Utpala dynast restored Kashmir's control over the Punjab and Afghanistan during the second half of the 9th and first quarter of the 10th Centuries AD. Later, the stylistic emphasis given to the Kashmiri style by the Hindu Shahis also penetrated into Siwalik, because by the end of the 10th Century AD, part of Kashmir from Laghman to Kangra acknowledged the rule of Jayapala of Waihand, who came to the Shahi throne in about 965 AD. Then, threatened in the west by the Ghazni rulers, he moved his capital to Bhatinda and probably also occupied the Kangra fort. Jayapala and his successors, however, could not stem the Muslim advance and were finally dispersed. Stylistic influences from Kashmir, were briefly important again in the early 11th Century AD, when Anantadeva of Kashmir overthrew Salvahana of Chamba (1028-60 AD), retaining power until the Lohara dynasty lost control and Kashmiri political as well as artistic hegemony declined for good. In the meantime, the state of Chamba having lost control over the Kullu valley, the state of Kullu under its rajas Santokhpal, Teghpal and Uchitpal rose to importance. The wealth and power of these kings even prompted them to attack Ladakh, Baltistan and perhaps Tibet. They were also great patrons of art and, according to tradition, gave shelter to the displaced artisans and craftsmen who fled before the advancing armies in the Indian plains, especially after Kanauj—then ruled by Rajyapala Pratihara—was taken by Mahmud of Ghazni (1018 AD). Through these refugees Pala models began to be brought into the hills in even greater numbers and finally succeeded in occupying a position no less important than that earlier held by examples of Kashmiri art. Examples of stone sculpture, perhaps executed during this period, are the images Vishnu, Ganesha and Mahishasuramardini in the niches of the Bajaura temple near Kullu. The slender but powerful bodies, the longish faces as well as the over-elongated limbs of the Pala art of this period are all to be observed in **Mahishasuramardini** (page 133). The sculpture seems to have been done by artisans from eastern India, as is shown by the marvellous sense of composition and volume to be seen in the arrangement of the arms and legs of the goddess and of the demon king, whom she has just overpowered. This is indicative of the renewed vitality and vigour of these refugee craftsmen in their new environment. The qualities of their work are also in keeping with the canon of ideal beauty of Meruvarman's brass figures. Like Meruvarman's images, the excessively slim yet elegant body of Mahishasuramardini is dressed in stylised costumes, and one can even make out the master touch

of Gugga's modelling by which the masses and surfaces, despite a pro-
fusion of details, are simplified and finished by slight engravings indicating lines and dots to represent transparency. But the small, elongated heads of the figures are more in tune with Pala sculptures than
with the rather bloated faces of Kashmiri tradition. The high crown
worn by the goddess is unlike the one adorning Shakti Devi of Chatrarhi,
but has three triangular corners of the type popular in Pala styles.
Especially remarkable is the hair, styled in a manner which is identical
with that seen in some of the paintings at Alchi in Ladakh, where the
ladies wear a carefully coiffured bun, the coils of which are bound

A RAJPUT PRINCESS,
NAGAR. 16th—17th CENTURY AD.

A COPPER MASK OF DEVI,
BHAKLI TEMPLE,
BHAKLI.16th—17th CENTURY AD.

A SILVER MASK OF DEVI,
BHAKLI TEMPLE,
BHAKLI. 16th—17th CENTURY AD.

A RAJPUT PRINCE, NAGAR. 16th—17th CENTURY AD.

together by pearls and various ornaments of colourful jewellery (pages 47, 58, 60, 61). In contrast, Gugga's Lakshana Devi has a high Jatamukta (crown of matted hair), more akin to the Gupta style.

Apart from these peculiarities, the theme of this sculpture is also one which repeatedly became a favourite in troubled times of war and conflict created by foreign invasions and internal strife. Confronted with danger, new manifestations of the god Shiva in his more demoniac appearance became supreme and Shiva's consort, "the great mother", was raised to even higher altars of worship in the form of Durga Mahishasuramardini, "slayer of the bull demon". The daughter of the Himalayan mountains is here seen in action against the powerful demon king, Mahishasura. who could transform his body into a buffalo in times of emergency. The demon king, after performing a severe penance, had obtained from Brahma the gift of immortality so that no male could kill him. Eventually, therefore, it was the goddess, a female, who vanquished him. Durga Devi is depicted here in the Pratyalidha attitude (which means that the left leg is outstretched while the right is bent) as she crushes the demon down to the ground, holding his hair in one of her left hands. In her other hands she holds a spear, a sword, a noose, a bow, an arrow, a Vajra (thunderbolt) and a cup made of a skull.

The consolidation of Pala style in the hills was gradual. Probably the indigenous craftsmen who took over from the refugee artists were slow to discard Kashmiri traditions in favour of Pala influences. This is especially noticeable in the moulding of secular figures, because here the craftsmen were less inhibited by the sensitive aesthetic theories or preordained clichés of scholastic theoreticians. In the depiction of ordinary life, the court influence of the rajas, ranis and their ministers was predominant and images of the donors formed an important part. One such example is **A Royal Personage** (page 129). Even though it is obviously based on the concept of elongated limbs of Pala art and Kashmiri stylisation, its lyrical quality nevertheless is inspired by a considerable freedom of expression exercised by the artists in the depiction of secular subjects. The exquisite arches formed by the two arms (like Karttikeya on page 134), the position of the hands with upturned palms one above the other, and the two hanging ends of the embroidered scarves symmetrically balancing the whole composition against the Torana (gate of honour) display an imagery which is certainly out of the ordinary. The radiating smile on the face is also quite unlike the affected and forced expressions of late Pala art or the early Pratihara style.

With the dissolution of the Pratihara empire, diverse stylistic influences began pouring in from western India. These were primarily the contribution of the Paramaras (c. 998-1260 AD), who were the first to break away from the Pratihara empire and become a paramount power in Malwa under Bhoja Dhara (c. 1010-55 AD). Also successors to the

Pratiharas were the Chandellas (*c.* 831-1202 AD) of Bundelkhand and the Kalachuris who, under Gangeyadeva (1030-41 AD) and Karna (1041-70 AD), became the leading powers of northern India. Then at Kanauj were established the Gahadavalas (*c* 1075-1200 AD) and in Ajmer the Chahamanas of Sambhar, who exercised a considerable influence until, led by Prithviraj III, they were defeated by the Muslims in 1192-3 AD. Several of these Rajput families, namely the Chauhans, the Paramaras and the Rathors, fled under the onslaught of Muhammad Ghori, who had by the end of the 12th Century AD established his advance military post at Multan in the Punjab. The stylistic tradition and artistic conventions brought in by these new arrivals were mainly the offshoots of the Pratihara art, but at the same time, in the courts of the Paramaras and Chandellas, influences outside the orbit of Pratihara style were also absorbed. Bilaspur (Bahlur), which is situated in the lower valley of the river Sutlej, is said by some people to have been founded by a cadet branch of the Chandellas of Bundelkhand.

The impact of these new ideas was, however, of limited value, primarily because of the absence of a centralised art patronage of the kind known during the earlier periods. With a few exceptions the Siwalik was now divided in a number of small principalities whose rulers had neither the will nor the resources to support new works of art. In this atmosphere the emphasis now shifted to the indigenous art style which, as already, mentioned, was ushered in by the early Pratihara art. The art of the Paramaras and Chandellas was also more in harmony with indigenous art style which, as alread mentioned, was ushered in by the early Pratihara art. The art of the Paramaras and Chandellas was also more in harmony with indigenous tastes and in the following period produced some very peculiar but most striking sculptures in stone. One such piece is **Vishnu and Lakshmi on Garuda** (page 131), in which can be seen a number of different influences—the elongated limbs of the Sena style, the sensuous display of Chandella sculpture, a crossbreeding of the powerful Chauhan faces and the bloated faces of Kashmiri art. Nevertheless, this charming sculpture on an eternal theme, by its bold departure from the accepted formulae, usherd in an era of Pahari style in sculpture mainly based on indigenous resources. **Kali Devi** (page 141) is another piece in which the solid objects take shape more in harmony with the block or the slab of stone out of which the figures are chiselled and in a style which is less inclined merely to repeat the clichés set by the accepted schools of medieval India. The emphasis in this style was on the natural shape of the stone, a tradition which emerged from the local practice of stone worship prevalent among most Himalayan communities. Even today, there are temples in this area and also in Nepal where the main deity in some shrines is no more than a piece of stone. Kali Devi (black goddess) was associated in Vedic times with Agni (fire) who had seven flickering tongues of flame for devouring oblations of butter. Of the

seven tongues, Kali was the most terrifying. Later, the goddess, also called Kalika, became the fierce consort of Shiva, who was himself worshipped as Mahadeva.

A beautiful image of **Mahadeva** (page 145) is now at Mandi in a private temple of the present Raja. Its massive vastness, pious and sturdy, its immovable and irrevocable bearing, primarily achieved by making the maximum use of the solidity and the shape of stone, epitomise the finest in the Pahari style of stone sculpture in this period.

Among the 14th Century AD pieces is an extraordinary sculpture in the Panchavaktra temple at Mandi, which is situated at the confluence of the river Beas and its tributaries and the Sutlej river. The image of **Pancha-anana Shiva** (page 118) is especially noteworthy. Its five faces are not placed in one row, as usually is the case (Karttikeya), but in such a way that the fourth face is on the reverse and the fifth on the top of the sculpture. The image is conceived somewhat like the Shikhara (tower) of a Hindu temple which, like the Buddhist Stupa, was interpreted as a sacrificial microcosm of the world. According to this concept, the plinth was regarded as an altar on which was built a superstructure representing the residence of gods, Mount Kailasha and the mythical mountain Meru. The all-seeing divine Yogi of the Himalaya, Shiva, with his consort Parvati, is here beautifully carved out of a mountain stone, whose gradations and alterations of relief painted in white effectively symbolise the snow-covered peaks of the Himalaya. The image of the red-eyed deity evokes a fantastic effect of the early red rays of the rising sun beyond the mountain summits, as the figure slowly emerges out of the darkness of the chapel of the temple.

The maturity of this indigenous style is particularly seen in a number of beautiful sculptures in the Triloknath temple in Mandi. Triloknath is identified with Shiva and this temple was built (1520 AD) by Sultan Devi, the pious queen of Raja Ajbar Singh. The chapel contains an almost life-size three-faced stone image of Shiva riding a bull with his consort Parvati in his lap. **Triloknath** (page 139) is a marvellous piece in which the sculptor, having refused to conform either to natural forms or to accepted models of established schools, successfully accomplished a masterpiece based on passionate remodelling of perspective. It is ranked among those pieces of ancient art which, though they touch the innermost chords of aesthetic sensibility in the modern mind, are not like the abstract sculptures of our own time, in which objects become slowly less recognisable. On the contrary, here is an attempt to portray divine forms based on the intense insight and spiritual scrutiny of the sculptor who was obviously haunted by the impossibility of imparting the attributes of an ever sharper symbolic meaning to his idols. Another most interesting sculpture done in the Pahari style is Shiva in the form of Ardhanari, half-female. **Shiva Ardhanari** (page 132) is the logical development of the trend which considered the male

MUSICIANS AND DANCERS AT A FESTIVAL.

to be the personification of the passive aspect, and the female the activating energy (Shakti). Though apparently opposite, they are essentially one and, as shown in this sculpture, literally transformed into one body of mystical union of the divine. The right half of this figure represents Shiva and the left Parvati. Shiva is portrayed with knotted hair, a serpent, a necklace of human skulls and holding musical instruments in his hands. The female half is seen wearing a diadem, an earring and a Nath (nose ring). Their respective Vahanas (vehicles) —the lion, counterpart of the goddess, and Nandi, Shiva's bull—are also represented by a curious animal with both bull and lion heads. In Siwalik, as in Nepal, the conjoint form of Shiva and Parvati and of Vishnu and Lakshmi as Ardhanaris gained popularity during this period. A natural corollary of this theme was also the cohesion of Shaivait and Vaishnavait iconometry in the form of Hari-Hara or Shankara-Narayana.

The most typical of the Siwalik's art forms, drawing their inspiration from the indigenous tradition of folk art, are the masks. These ageless images are undoubtedly the most fantastic and formidable art link in the entire Himalaya. The masks represent the Himalayan atmosphere of awe-inspiring mighty peaks and deep-sounding river gorges, of eerie rustlings of haunted forest leaves in the valleys and desert-like mirages appearing among the giant mountain landscapes. When the cult of the Devi captured the people's imagination, and more and more temples were erected in almost every hamlet, these masks were in great demand because the local temples which could not afford to commission a complete idol of the goddess could still do her honour through such symbols. With the passage of time, the practice became a custom so that even when the temples were more prosperous and their imagery more resplendent, masks still occupied the principal altar—and were no longer made of wood or clay, as in the past, but cast or beaten in metals such as copper, silver and even gold. **Copper Mask of Devi** (page 137) and **Silver Mask of Devi** (page 137) are two such beautiful examples. The silver mask, with an inscription "Devi" on the lower right-hand corner and the name of the artist (or perhaps the donor) "Vaithalmal" on the left, projects a face which is typically that of a Gaddi. For almost a millennium the Gaddi tribe formed a separate ethnic enclave, although they adopted the religion and the dialect of the western Pahari area. The Gaddis are gay and cheerful nomads who live in small villages in the upper Beas valley in the snowy ranges of Dhauladhar and Pir Panjal. They are hardy and adventurous people who love fun and excitement and never miss an opportunity to participate in festivals, such as the annual Kullu fair. Since time immemorial, on occasions such as these, masks of the Devi were paraded in the streets in processions of decorated chariots. The copper mask on page 137 is also a remarkable indication of changing styles in a crucial period, when the art in these regions was gradually becoming the exclusive province of Rajput influences. In the face of the copper piece can be seen characteristic Rajput features adorned with ornaments which even today can be seen in several areas of Rajasthan. The bas-relief of the silver mask has been considerably lifted so that the sophisticated face in copper is by comparison full and more natural.

In the Indo-Gangetic plains, systematic destruction of idols and internecine wars among the Rajput aristocracy accelerated the disappearance in the 13th Century AD of the civilisation of medieval India, but its art tradition in one form or another was kept alive in the Himalaya, preserved in its indigenous culture. Unlike the stone sculptures in the indigenous style and the ageless symbols, the masks, there is no early example of wall paintings. Painting in the folk tradition seems, however, to have always flourished in a folk style, as indicated by examples such as **Durga** (page 147). This is among several paintings depicted on the walls of an ancient temple at the Bhakli village, on the road between Mandi and Kullu. Its folk character is evident from its rather naive depiction of the legend. Folk art iconography did not strictly follow the various theological and stylistic rules and therefore did not

MAHADEVA, PRIVATE TEMPLE OF RAJA OF MANDI, HIMACHAL PRADESH. 15th CENTURY AD.

have a distinct meaning as in the past when the standard of Sanskrit scholarship was higher. It was more an expression of reconstructed imagery whose conventions were hardly understood. Mistakes in iconography were common and often the artists invented their own style or followed their own imagination. In northern India, the art of painting for quite some time was reduced to the copying of the standard Jain text, the *Kalpasutra,* by Jain merchants working under the new masters but building temples in lonely and far off places and secretly commissioning miniature paintings. These were more decorative and ornamental than "expressionist". This antiquarian style appears to have received a considerable fillip under the powerful Rajput federation of the 15th Century AD. As a result, new tendencies towards variations from the Jain *Kalpasutra* style became evident in Gujaratr manuscripts, such as the *Vasantavilasa* and *Balagopalastuti* and later the more popular *Devi Mahatmya*. Nevertheless, this renaissance was shortlived, not so much because of suppressive activity on the part of the new rulers, but more as a result of the Hindu Vaishnava reform movements, which increasingly caught the imagination of the people. In fact, the prevalence of Islam promoted this trend, as Muslim monotheism, and particularly Sufi mysticism, propagated similar ideas of equality among all men before one God. In the 12th Century AD, the theology of access to God's boundless love and mercy irrespective of social status was already expounded by Shaiva Lingayats and the Vaishnava leaders, Ramanuja and Madhavacharya, but in terms of art its impact was felt only when these ideas were elaborated in the language of the people through poems, such as *Gita Govinda* which Jayadeva composed in the court of Lakshmanasena (1179-1205 AD). In an allegorical style the poet narrated the loves of Radha and Krishna, striving to escape the temptation of the flesh and seeking to achieve a mystical union with God. In the 14th Century AD, these ideals were consolidated by the Vaishnava reformer, Ramananda, and the 15th and 16th Centuries AD saw a wave of mystic emotion preached by Vidyapati, Chandi Das, Chaitanya, Vallabhacharya, Mirabai, Kabir, Nanak and several others. Examples of its artistic expression are the 16th Century AD manuscripts *Laur-Chanda* and *Chaurapanchasika*. The oldest known manuscript, *The Bhagavata Purana*, illustrated in a style which is broadly termed "Rajput", was painted in 1538 AD, but it was not until late in the 17th Century AD that this style became popular in the Siwalik.

Meanwhile, new elements of style introduced by the Moghul emperors also began to infiltrate the Sialik ranges. The origin of this trend can be traced to 1525 AD when Babur, originally the Himurid ruler of Ferghana, Samarkand and then of Kabul, established his authority in northern India after overpowering the two great powers, the Rajput Ranas of Mewar and the Lodhi Sultans. His son, Humayum (1530-56 AD), a great art lover like his father, seems to have introduced large-

size illustrations to the *Hamza Nama*, a text describing the fabulous adventure story of Amir Hamza's conquest of the heathens. Amir Hamza was an uncle of the Prophet Muhammad. Purely Persian in style at first, these paintings soon absorbed scenes from Indian village life, Indian costumes and jewellery, even Hindu idols. With the expansion of the empire into Malwa, Rajputana, Gujarat and Bengal, a new cultural revolution set in which, having overcome resistance from the earlier schools of art, finally succeeded in occupying an important position.

As in the past, there was a considerable time-lag before this eclectic style was claimed in the hills of the Siwalik region. Its impact was perhaps felt for the first time at Basohli, an ancient state on the bank of the Ravi. During the reign of Raja Kirpal Pal (1678-95 AD), an artist, Devi Dasa, painted the manuscript of the *Rasamanjari* in 1694-5 AD. *Rasamanjari* is an erotic treatise devoted to male and female written by the poet Bhanudatta in the 15th Century AD.

The abortive campaigns and unpopular policies of the Moghul emperor, Aurangzeb, caused disintegration throughout his empire and central control was further loosened after his death early in the 18th Century AD. This decline does not, however seem to have had the same strong impact on Pahari art as did the sack of Delhi in 1739 AD by Nadir Shah. After 1739, an abrupt change of style is noticeable in the hills, apparently the work of artists trained in Moghul painting in the court of Muhammad Shah (1719-48 AD). Such families of artists migrated in large numbers to seek employment with new patrons in the comparative safety and more settled conditions of life in the hills. As described elsewhere, a situation such as this occurred in past centuries too, but this time the suddenness of the change in style suggests that the diversion of the "great royal highway" through the Siwalik was an additional and important factor. Previously the route commonly used had run through Taxila and Lahore, but now, with upheaval and insecurity in the plains, a more difficult but safer trade route was followed through Bilaspur, Nadaun, Guler, Nurpur, Basohli, Jammun and so up to Srinagar in Kashmir. It was this ancient trade route which, in the 8th Century AD, was also instrumental in happy cultural intercourse between the territories of Meruvarman's Trigarta and Lalitaditya's Kashmir. Now, as in the past, merchants established new centres at several points along the route, bringing greater prosperity and more intimate cultural contact between these regions.

The local hereditary chieftains, taking advantage of the declining Moghul empire to recover most of their ancestral territories, were now in a better position to extend their patronage to the newly-arrived artists. The result was that, by the middle of the 18th Century AD, an unprecedented art activity blossomed in practically all the hill states. Benefactors of the arts in Jammu were Ranjit Dev and his youngest brother Balwant Singh (1735-81 AD); Umed Singh (1748-64 AD) and Raj Singh

A DANCING BEAR AT A FESTIVAL.

(1764-94 AD) were cultured patrons in Chamba; Ghamand Chand (1751-74 AD) gave shelter to artists in Kangra; and in Bilaspur the reign of Devi Chand (1741-78 AD) produced some remarkable paintings. Among these powerful centres of art it was, curiously enough, at tiny Guler, a politically insignificant state, that the second important phase of Pahari painting began in the reign of Govardhan Chandt (c. 1745-73 AD). Appropriately called the Guler style, its early schools possibly secured the patronage and support of the merchants trading through Guler, situated as it was on the new trade route. Later, this small principality was absorbed by Kangra, which is the reason why this style, covering a period of three decades or so from about 1740-70 AD, is also called the pre-Kangra style.

Towards the end of the reign of Ghamand Chand, the Kangra group of states consisting of Kangra, Guler and Chamba became tributaries of the Sikhs who were beginning to assert themselves. Later, the Sikhs withdrew from the hills and in 1786 AD Sansar Chand became the leader of the Trigarta group. Thus, the style of painting flourishing in

A VIEW OF THE RIVER BEAS FROM THE TRILOKNATH TEMPLES, MANDI.

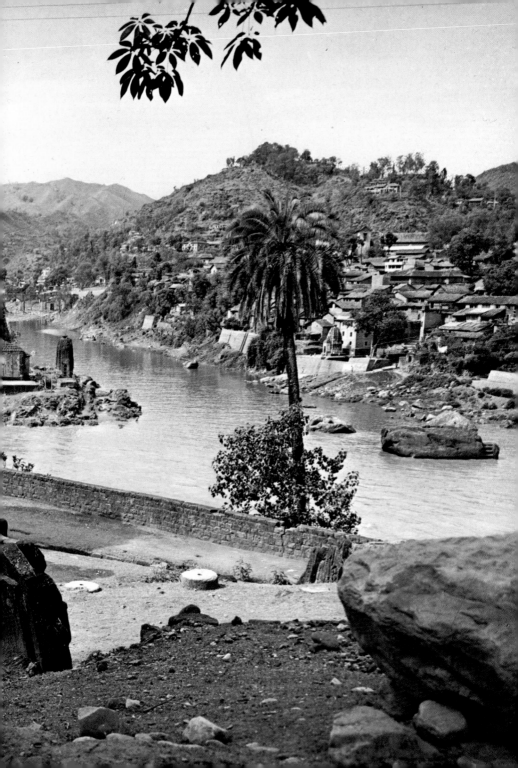

the hills from 1770 AD to the end of Sansar Chand's reign in the 19th Century AD is, by common consent, called the Kangra style.

These comments on miniature paintings are equally applicable to Pahari murals—the wall-paintings were merely tracing of these miniatures on the larger surfaces of walls. The surviving murals in the hills are at Jammu, Chamba, Aki, Dadasiba. Dharamsala, Dhamthal, Kanthal, Nadaun, Nurpur, Sujanpur Tira, Mandi and Kullu and these do not go back earlier than the 19th Century AD. A few exceptions are some of the lovely wall-paintings inside the Rang Mahal of Chamba (since removed to the National Museum in New Delhi) some of which on stylistic grounds can perhaps be dated in the third quarter of the 18th Century AD.

Chamba never regained the cultural zenith of Meruvarman's period. Attempts to restore its past glories of artistic tradition by Prithvi Singh (c. 1641 AD) and again in the middle of the 18th Century by Umed Singh (1748-64 AD) were at best pale reflections. Umed Singh's greatest achievement was the Rang Mahal (palace of colour) at Chamba, a fortress-like residence with gardens, which was inspired by Moghul architecture. The palace was later considerably extended and modified by his successors, Raj Singh (1764-94 AD), Jit Singh (1794-1808 AD) and Charat Singh (1804-44 AD).

One of the loveliest murals is **Krishna Lila** (pages 126-7), which depicts episodes from Krishna's varied and colourful life. The wall-painting is infused with a developed sense of romantic landscape, based on the mountain flora and the artist's everyday observation of common village life. The balanced colour combinations, fluid drawing and perfect placing of the groups of men and women devotees, as well as the delicacy and tenderness of their expressions, all recall the best of the late Guler style. This work was probably commissioned by Raj Singh, as is evident if we compare it with one of the raja's own portraits, in which he is watching a girl dancing (late N. C. Mehta collection) and which has been closely dated to 1772 AD. Notwithstanding the element of coarseness which was inevitable in drawings done with a steeple brush on walls, this beautiful mural, like Raj Singh's portrait, has all the refinement of composition, drawing and colouring of the period of transition from Guler to Kangra style. An indication of this is the standard Kangra-type profiles, which according to Karl Khandalawala mean "the nose almost in line with the forehead, long narrow eyes and sharp chin, no modelling of the face and the hair treated as a flat black mass with no shading". As against this, in the Bhagavata type, which was an offshoot of the Guler style, one sees that "the face is well modelled and shaded so judiciously that it possesses an almost porcelain-like delicacy. The nose is small and slightly upturned and the hair is carefully painted". The latter group includes some of the finest of the Pahari miniatures, such as a *Gita Govinda* and a *Satsaiya*, to be seen in the Tehri Garhwal Darbar collection, a *Ragamala*, now in the National Museum in New Delhi, and of course the *Bhagvata Purana*, after which the female type takes its epithet.

Apart from the Guler and Kangra influences, other paintings inspired by almost every tendency of style in the hills indicate that these were done by several artists not only at different times, but also in the same period. This further substantiates the view that, in the 18th Century AD, there was in the hills a group of artists who, unlike artists in the Moghul courts, did not owe complete allegiance to individual patrons. This tendency was probably encouraged by the increase in the number of patrons of equal status and also by the ease of travel along the re-opened Siwalik trade route. Pandit Seu, for example, was a refugee artist from Kashmir or the plains and he settled in Jasrota about 1740 AD. His younger son, Nainsukh, whose reputation rests on paintings of Balwant Singh at Jammu (1748 AD), apparently also painted at Guler.

Women on a Swing (page 154) is a delightful mural which appears to be inspired by the important school of painting flourishing in Kahlur (Bilaspur). This state is situated in the lower Sutlej valley and is said to have been founded by a cadet branch of the Chandellas of Bundelkhand. Bilaspur enjoyed great prosperity in Devi Chand's reign (1771-8 AD), being the first halting station on the newly opened trade route to Kashmir. Because of its greater contact with the plains, the Bilaspur school of painting exhibits a stronger accent not only in its transformation of the Moghul style, but also in its similarity, however remote, to such qualities of Chandella art as its sweeping rhythm and seductive sensuality. The carefree atmosphere and joyful mood of this painting also reflect the happier days of the Moghul courts, depicting a style of life which was a curious mixture of Moghul, Indo-Islamic and Rajput habits. In fact, these forms were originally outlined in the studios established by Akbar the Great (1556-1605 AD), where artists such as Mir Sayyid Ali and Abdas-Samad, whom Humayun had brought from the Persian court of Shah Talimasap I, trained Indian novices. Akbar, having married Rajput princesses, among them a pupil of the Vaishnava saint-singer Mira Bai, established close links with the Rajputs and their art. In its charm of composition and lighthearted mood, this painting, like many others subsequently done in the hills, is reminiscent of some of the illustrations of the famous *Akbar-nama* (now in the Victoria and Albert Museum, London) and *Razm-nama* at Jaipur, which are among the several epics, romances and didactic books, painted in Akbar's court. On the other hand, the Chandella manner is betrayed by sensuality of drawing created by sweeping lines recalling the uninhibited contours and seductive frivolity of Chandella sculptures. The artist here has marvellously succeeded in giving that extra movement to the Women on a Swing by sweeping colours and the lines of their garments. The painting, as well as other murals in the Rang Mahal belonging to the late period, have so many intermingled stylistic influences that is is impossible to separate one element from the other.

Here, for instance, even if the artist was inspired by the Bilaspur manner, the women have become merely another version of the Kangra style.

Another painting also deriving its inspiration from the Bilaspur manner of the late period is **Shiva-Parvati** (page 156). The deities are seen here on a tiger skin in the vicinity of mount Kailasha. Shiva has his elephant-headed son, Ganesha, on his lap, while Karttikeya with six heads is seated beside him. The bull Nandi, the vehicle on which Devi rides, and even the little rat which is Ganesha's vehicle, are all drawn in a manner by which the third dimension is represented by juxtaposition of figures of different sizes. As in the Pahari paintings of the end of the 18th Century AD, there is no attempt at modelling or a conventional third dimensional perspective. This mural, too, had its antecedents in the miniature painting, but in the process of translation, new factors, such as the use of a steeple brush and enlarging the area and figures, produced results which are in perfect harmony with the intended purpose of interior decoration. The large spaces of monocolour which the artist used to achieve the interlocking of surfaces have created an organic unity, which is quite different from that achieved by the miniatures where the colours had to be meticulously filled in. The contrasts thus achieved are more spectacular, submerging, in a riot of colour, such anomalies of style as the delicate flowers of the draperies set beside the heavy strokes of the brush which colour the dense foliage of the trees, mountains and sky.

A mixture of different Pahari styles is also seen in **Narasimha Avatara** (page 157). Even though this subject was very popular during the medieval period, it is painted in a manner which is quite independent of any of its medieval prototypes. The flat yet glowing colours are here essentially filled in, the figures are forced and expressionless except for the hypnotic eyes. In keeping with the Indo-Islamic style of decorative floral motifs, the major part of the backdrop is filled in with bright patterns of textile design and the central part of the picture is surrounded by borders meticulously charged with foliage and creepers as well as other designs plainly borrowed from Moghul art. The Torana (gate of honour) has given way to a more elaborate inner outline of the main entrance of a mosque, even though the subject belongs to Hindu mythology. It depicts Narasimha (the man-lion), a form which Vishnu assumed in order to deliver the world from the tyranny of the demon Hiranyakasipu.

Examples of the last phase of Pahari wall-painting are seen in **Radha and Krishna** (page 158) and **A Rani's Portrait** (page 159). With facial expressions possibly borrowed from Guler through Kangra, while the ornaments and the head of Krishna recall the Basohli manner, these murals are obviously a hotchpotch of varied influences and display a rapidly diminishing range of colour and a coarsening of the line and composition of the Kangra style. The original vitality, expressiveness

and freshness of the early Kangra manner have here given way to forced facial expressions, mechanically produced by such common devices as upturned corners of the lips to produce a smile. The murals are inside one of the palaces of the Rajas of Mandi: this was used as a harem and the murals were conceived, as always, to serve as interior decorations. Nevertheless, even in their decline the paintings are a good indication of what this art must have been in its youth if examples of the earlier periods had survived. Evidence suggests that Mandi was once a favourite resort for the families of traditional painters. The names of one Sajnu, a Hindu, and a Muslim painter, Mohammadi, occur among the artists who are said to have come from the court of Sansar Chand to reside in Mandi.

NARASIMHA AVATARA,
RANG MAHAL PALACE,
CHAMBA.
EARLY 19th CENTURY AD

SHIVA-PARVATI, RANG MAHAL PALACE, CHAMBA. EARLY 19th CENTURY AD.   157

RADHA AND KRISHNA, RAJA'S HAREM IN THE MANDI
PALACE, MANDI. 19th CENTURY AD.

A RANI'S PORTRAIT, RAJA'S HAREM IN THE MANDI
PALACE, MANDI. 19th CENTURY AD.

NEPAL

Nepal is the proud possessor of the highest mountain summit in the world, Mount Everest. This colourful and beautiful country, an area of roughly 141,000 square meters on the southern slopes of the Himalaya, extends for about 900 kilometers between Nanda Devi (7,817 meters) in the west and Kanchenjunga (8,578 meters) in the east. This elongated rectangle averages about 160 kilometers in width and contains a tremendous variety of terrains and climates, ranging from the arctic conditions of the eternal snows of the higher regions through the arid wastes of the high Tibetan plateau to the tropical forests of the Ganges plain.

The northern frontiers of Nepal do not invariably follow the great Himalayan crest-line and some narrow strips of Nepalese territory lie in the trans-Himalayan zone to the north of the southern Himalayan watershed. These northern areas are linked to the rest of Nepal by deep, precipitous gorges and formidable passes cutting towards the south across the ranges. The most westerly is the Taklakot pass (4,876 meters) crossing the Nepal-Tibet border at Khojarnath on the upper reaches of the Humla branch of the river Karnali. Above Muktinath and beyond the Kali headwaters is the Mustang pass. There is also the Kyerong, a low river pass on which ponies can be used, and the Kuti pass, which lies beyond Kodari on the upper Sun Kosi river and, being the main route to Lhasa, is of considerable importance. Just west of Mount Everest is the Nangpa pass (5,792 meters) and further east following the course of the river Arun is the Hatiya pass. There is also the Walungchun pass lying below the western shoulder of Kanchenjunga. To the south of the Great Himalaya and almost parallel to it is the Mahabharat chain of mountains running from west to east across almost the entire country and forming a natural barrier of peaks some of which are as high as 3,000 meters. The Mahabharat mountain passes are formed by the intersection of southward flowing rivers—the Seti, Rapti, Gandak, Bhagmati and mighty Arun Kosi—which emerge into the Ganges plain at an altitude of no more than 200 to 500 meters. The differences in altitude between the mountain peaks and the river beds being enormous, these wild gorges are a scene of awe-inspiring yet enchanting beauty as the rapids debouch in the Siwalik zone of foothills. These hills are about 1,500 meters in height and, unlike the Siwaliks of the Himachal Pradesh, mostly merge directly into the higher ranges of the Mahabharat chain. Further south, situated between the foothills and the Indian frontier, is a narrow strip of lovely country called the Terai, which is nowhere more than about 45 kilometers in width and only about 200 meters above sea-level.

Apart from the Terai, the most habitable regions of Nepal are the central lands which lie between the giants of the Great Himalaya in the north and the Mahabharat chain of mountains towards the south. Between these two ramparts is a tract, 60 to 100 kilometers wide at an elevation of 600 to 2,000 meters, extending from the frontier with the Indian Kumaon district in the west to the borders of Sikkim towards the east. The region is divided into nine natural divisions by the wide valleys of the transverse rivers and their tributaries. The midlands are interrupted also by occasional higher lying zones, so that the valleys, such as that of Kathmandu (1,400 meters), appear like saucers surrounded by hills rising from 2,000—3,000 meters in height. The people of Nepal exhibit an enormous racial variety. One finds men of fair complexion and tall stature with long heads and prominent noses living together in the same locality with dark, short-statured people with broad heads, flat noses and oblique eyes. The process of racial admixture seems to have continued over thousands of years and is due mainly to the immigration of the Indo-Aryan and Mongoloid races. While in some areas such as the Kathmandu valley, Pokhara and Dhankuta, the intermingling has brought forth a unique new culture which is typically Nepalese, in other places distinct racial strains can still be clearly distinguished. Nonetheless, in the course of time all immigrants into Nepal have identified themselves with Nepalese aspirations, however distant their racial origins. Among them are the Khas from Central Asia and, later, the western Himalaya, the Shakyas of Kapilavastu, the Mallas of Pava and Kusinagara (now Gorakhpur), the Lichhavis of Vaisali, and the Karnatas of Simraongarh (originally of Karnataka or Maharashtra). Similarly the Thakalis, Gurungs and other groups of Mongoloid origin were in course of time assimilated into Nepalese society.

Like other Himalayan peoples, the Nepalese, and especially their artists, found that the hard facts of Himalayan topography and history could only be understood in the light of the endless and fantastic legends based on mythology, mostly of Indian origin. For example, a legend tells us that "The valley on the southern side of the snowy range, which is within Sumeru (Himalaya), was formerly known as Nag Hrad or the tank of the serpent, until it was drained by a single cut of the sword of Bodhisattva Manjushri to form the present fertile valley". This legend is obviously of Buddhist origin and comparatively recent, because images of Bodhisattva Manjushri are not found in the Gandhara and Mathura schools of sculpture and neither is the Bodhisattva mentioned in the works of Ashvaghosa, Nagarjuna or Aryadeva. On the other hand, it is very likely that the message of Buddhism had already crossed into the Nepal valley shortly after the birth of Gautama, the Buddha (567 BC) in Kapilavastu on the India-Nepal border. Definite evidence of this is, first, the inscribed memorial pillar at Lumbini which was erected by the emperor Ashoka in commemoration of his pilgrimage to the birthplace of the master and, secondly, Stupas of the original shape, four at Lalitpatan and one at Kirtipur in the Kathmandu valley. Tradition also has it that Ashoka's daughter, Charumati, married the Kshatriya Devpala and later set up a Vihara or monastery in Deopatan called Chabahal, which she entered to become a Buddhist nun.

Recent archaeological excavations at Tilaurakot, Beniarahi and Paisia in the Terai have indicated that there was civilisation in this region before 300 BC. **A Terracotta Head** (page 167) from Benjarahi, near Lumbini, the birthplace of the Buddha, is an interesting example. On the basis of comparable finds in the Indian Ganges plain, the cultural influences of the Mauryas and the Sungas during the three centuries before Christ penetrated the Nepalese Terai, even though the limited excavations at Hadigao, Lajimpat and Dhum Varahi in the Kathmandu valley have not so far indicated settlements earlier than the period of the Nepal-Lichhavis in the early centuries of the Christian era.

Nepali *Vamshavalis*, or genealogical records of the rulers, are eloquent about a Kiranti dynasty said to be the earliest rulers of Nepal. Limbu and Rais people even today call themselves Kirantis. More evidence, however, is available regarding the heritage of the Lichhavis who are mentioned in Buddhist literature as well as in the *Manusmriti*. This great republican tribe, with their capital at Vaisali in the Ganges plain, were in alliance even in the time of king Bimbisara with the Magadha kings ruling from Rajagriha. Bimbisara, with whom Gautama Buddha had established contact before he achieved enlightenment, later became one of Buddha's disciples. Vaisali, the capital of the Lichhavis before they settled in Nepal, is alluded to in the *Ramayana* and its foundation is ascribed to Ikshvaku, the ancestor of Rama. Mahariva, the Jain prophet, was claimed by Vaisali as one of her citizens and Buddha's intimate associations with this city are well known.

In the *Dhammapada* there is a mention of a Lichhavi youth named Mahali who, after finishing his education at Taxila, devoted his life to educating his people. When the Lichhavis established themselves in Nepal, their students, artists and craftsmen thus apparently continued to travel using the "great royal highway", precursor of the grand trunk road in India. The universities of Taxila, Ujjain and Varanashi were famous from the earliest times and these were connected by this highway to Pataliputra, only a few kilometers from Vaisali. Pataliputra, founded by Ajatasatru on the bank of the river Ganges in the 5th Century BC, had become world famous. The golden palace of the king in the centre of the town is stated by Megasthenes to have been "more splendid than the palaces of Sura and Ecbatana". The *Kathasarit Sagara*, which contains the statement of Gunadhya (1st Century BC), mentions Pataliputra as the home of culture, learning and the fine arts. The Ashokan pillars at Lumbini, Nigalisagar and Kudan are the earliest examples of stone carving within the bounds of Nepal, going back to the middle of the 3rd Century BC. The Lichhavis were the fortunate inheritors of this tradition which even during the changed circumstances of the Christian era, was carried on uninterrupted in the partial seclusion of the Nepal valley. The earliest inscriptional references to the Lichhavis occur on the coins of Chandragupta I, who married Kumara Devi, a Lichhavi princess. In fact, it was with the help of this

A *LOKESHVARA*, PATAN, NEPAL, LATE PERIOD.

powerful republican tribe that the Guptas established themselves in Magadha and subsequently became a paramount Indian power. Chandragupta's son and successor, Samudragupta (328—76 AD), was responsible for the famous inscription on a pillar at Allahabad describing Nepal as a border kingdom in his time. Nepal was probably ruled at that time by Vrishadeva, who according to the *Vamshavalis* was the great grandfather of king Manadeva. Some scholars consider that, but for a brief interval of about 70 years (576 AD to about 641 AD) when the Thakuris under Amshuvarman and Jishnu Gupta respectively controlled the valley, the Lichhavis ruled Nepal (400—750 AD) contemporaneously with the imperial Guptas and their successor states in India. This is partly why stone sculptures that are clearly attributed to the Lichhavi period in many respects greatly resemble Gupta prototypes. A marvellous limestone sculpture, **A Royal Personage** (page 180), is a remarkable link in the style of art which can already be seen developing on the stupa of Bharhut (2nd Century BC) and in the art of Mathura during the first three centuries of the Christian era. During these five centuries the rather heavy and clumsy figures of Yakshas and Yakshis, spirits of trees and nature, gradually grew into vigorous sculptures as they became part of the local country cults assimilated by Buddhism, especially the Buddhist school of Mathura. Under the influence of the art of north-west India, the Mathura statues in turn had absorbed and transformed some, but not all, of the iconographical conventions of Gandhara, among them the folds of garments and the plain circular nimbus. All these characteristics are seen in the figure of a Royal Personage, which appears to be stylistically suspended between the hieratically rigid, snub-nosed figures, which are carved in low relief on the stone blocks of Bharhut's gates and railings, and the impressively conceived, fully-modelled Mathura sculptures. This piece is partly a bas-relief and partly fully modelled and stands firmly in the Samabhanga (erect pose). It greatly resembles the Mathura Bodhisattva (now in the archaeological museum at Sarnath) holding a tassel of drapery with the left hand. The elbows, making two symmetrical arches with the hands almost touching the hips, convey an extraordinary feeling of strength. This atmosphere is accentuated by the broad chest and shoulders, the robustness of the limbs and the majestic posture. Like the Sarnath Buddha sculptures, this figure possesses an extraordinary vitality, even though the body is moulded in a kind of geometrical abstraction of combined spherical and rounded shapes. The sculptor has fully succeeded in infusing a strong character of integrity which inspires confidence and dependence.

The development of Nepali art from this period onward can be roughly followed by examining the formation of the Mathura school of art first under Kushan patronage and then gradually reaching its apogee under the imperial Guptas and their successor states. The Lichhavis, who had assisted the Gupta's ascent to power, appear to have greatly benefited

A TERRACOTTA HEAD, BENJARAHI, NEPAL. 3rd CENTURY BC.

from the increasing wealth and strength of this dynasty. The Gupta's ambition to bring about the political unification of India had in turn stimulated a flowering of ancient Indian culture in all its varied fields, religious and literary as well as artistic. In the Nepal valley, too, this development did not go unnoticed and there was an analogous national upsurge and a corresponding renaissance in the arts. The Lichhavis, though Vaishnavas, allowed their subjects to follow the religion of the Buddha. This tradition has continued to the present day and is clearly demonstrated in the division of the talented Newar craftsmen into Shiva-margis, or followers of Shiva, and Buddhamargis, or followers of the Buddha, both groups living happily together.

Images of important Hindu deities which were created in the Udaigiri caves in Malwa during the first years of Chandragupta's campaigns against the Mahakshatrapas of Ujjain included representations of Narayana, Durga, Ganesha, Mukhalinga, Skanda and especially the gigantic Varaha (the boar incarnation of Vishnu) raising the earth goddess from the chaos. The legend of Dasavatara, or the ten incarnations of Vishnu, was known even in the pre-Christian era, but in art it became very popular during this time. Varaha is also seen in Nepal in a style which on first sight is rather crude and brutal. This is understandable because, as Stella Kramrisch rightly pointed out, "The shapes in which the Newars venerated their own divinities, which had preceded the gods of Buddhism and Hinduism in Nepal, sharply differed from the forms of the latter. Stones were venerated in their natural shapes, whether singly, piled in heaps under trees, raised on altars or still in the ground below the surface of the earth. Such *objets trouvés* were numerous but they did not arouse the visual imagination, did not clamour for precise limits, proportions, or similarity to anything. It is only when the gods of India in their Indian form came to Nepal that the history of Nepali art began".

Varaha (page 184) at Dhum Varahi in the Kathmandu valley was conceived at a period when the Gupta Hindu iconography was still developing and its religious imagery had not gone beyond the experimental stages. It was a difficult concept to interpret because, in the absence of established guide-lines, the artists had to depend largely on their own resources while exploring the potentialities of depicting the animal form through the medium of the human body. Nevertheless, the sculptors in the picturesque setting at Dhum Varahi have made full and effective use of the stone and have succeeded in creating a sturdy, powerful deity, capable of lifting the weight of the earth on his left elbow. The legend tells of a demon named Hiranyaksa who had dragged the earth to the bottom of the sea. Vishnu, when requested to recover the earth, assumed the form of a boar and, after a struggle of a thousand years, slew the demon and rescued her. By the time that this sculpture was made, the combined man-animal form became as

VISHNU VIKRANTAMURTI, KATHMANDU, NEPAL. 467 AD.

popular in Nepal as the woman and tree configuration and the man and woman couple.

An early sculpture of this period in the Varaha style is **Vainteya** (page 222) or the sun-eagle Garuda at Changu Narayan. According to an inscription by Manadeva, this sculpture belongs to the year equivalent to 464 AD. Even in its attitude of extreme humility and submission to the heavenly king Vishnu, the massive figure of Vainteya is endowed with great energy and strength. This quality and expression of power is so overwhelming that the onlooker may well overlook the shortcomings of the sculpture.

As revealed by the elegant and ornate style of Chandragupta's coins after his conquest of Ujjain, the classical Gupta style came to the forefront at the Gupta court in the first half of the 5th Century. At this time, also, the tightly curled hair styles and the elaborate costumes and ornaments associated with the Gupta influence first appear. In Nepal this style is seen for the first time in two inscribed pieces of Vishnu as a dwarf changing his form into that of **Vishnu Vikrantamurti** (page 169), in order to cover the whole universe in three steps. This lovely bas-relief is inscribed with the date equivalent to 467 AD and dedicated by the Lichhavi, Manadeva, to his mother Rajavati. It displays all those features of the classical style by which works of art were essentially conceived in a theatrical idiom. In keeping with the instructions contained in the *Vishnudharmottaram* that "sculpture and painting cannot be understood without a knowledge of dancing", this bas-relief is its true expression. Faithful to the tradition, and despite its masterly sense of rhythm and harmony shewn by gestures and poses based on dance movements, the result is far from being naturalistic. It essentially projects a vision which, in keeping with Yoga practices, is on an aesthetic plane—the ecstatic union of the spiritual with the material world. The somewhat harsh imitation of the Mathura school and even the deficiencies of the late offshoots of the Sunga style have disappeared, giving rise to a lyrical idealisation of classical standards. The abrupt change of style between the inscribed Vainteya figure (464 AD) and the Vishnu Vikrantamurti sculpture (467 AD) is one of the most intriguing aspects of Nepalese art history. The intervening time is very short and the stylistic gap too great to be explained away either by a process of progressive specialisation or by the idiosyncratic styles of the individual sculptors. Its explanation once again lies in a fundamental and recurring phenomenon: Himalayan art benefited from the turmoils and uncertainties of its neighbourhood. The case in point here was the termination in about 466 AD of the reign of the Indian emperor Skandagupta and the obscurity of the ensuing decade. In the confusion of the ten years that followed the end of Skandagupta's rule (even though the imperial Guptas continued to reign until 530 AD) a number of artists and craftsmen seem to have taken refuge beyond the Mahabharat range in the Kathmandu valley. That these newcomers were obviously proficient in the art style patronised by the imperial Guptas is reflected in the expertise and in the marvellous sense of rhythm and action seen in the Vishnu Vikrantamurti sculpture. This also explains the stylistic disparity between the Vishnu Vikrantamurti sculpture reproduced here and the identically inscribed and dated

NARASIMHA AVATARA, CHANGU NARAYAN, NEPAL. 12th—13th CENTURY AD.

Vishnu Vikrantamurti frieze at Tilganga near the Pashupatinath temple. Conjectural as it is, it is probable that while the former was sculptured by refugee artists, the Tilganga sculpture is a product of Nepalese craftsmen, who had yet mastered this new style. It was, however, not long before the talented Neari sculptors not only fully absorbed the

171

techniques of Gupta mannerism but even surpassed their teachers in the course of the following two centuries.

On the basis of the available data, the period of about two centuries from the execution of the two Vishnu Vikrantamurtis in 467 AD to the end of king Amshuvarman's reign in 621 AD is the most creative period of Nepalese contribution to the plastic arts. The declining "golden age" of the Gupta renaissance in India was revived and recreated here by the sensitive and competent hands of Nepalese sculptors. Their thorough and intelligent grasp of the essential principles of art and its true aims, their highly developed aesthetic sense and masterly handling of the stone, produced some exquisite sculptures. Nepali artists took maximum advantage of the techniques evolved at the great art "laboratories" of the Guptas, such as those at Mathura and Sarnath, where centuries of effort and experimentation had perfected a distinct type of ideal beauty. The experimental period was now over, and the zenith of classical artistic splendour was about to begin. Its characteristic was the supremacy and dominance of man, in control of his destiny and of wealth and love, so that even the deities were moulded as supermen, though on a higher level of existence.

Among the pieces depicting Hindu legends, a beautiful example at Changu Narayan is **Vishnu Vishvarupa** (page 175), which is mentioned in a Jishnugupta inscription. Done in the high classical Gupta style, its theatrical representation pulsating with life and vibrating movement is comparable with the well-known Ananta Shayin relief (500 AD) in the Gupta temple at Deogarh in central India. The crowded scene is filled with an incredible variety of poses and gestures and even in this limited space the host of deities seem to move about freely and elegantly. In this phantasmagoria the supreme god Vishnu is shown "wearing all forms, omnipresent and universal". The episodes are interwoven with great ingenuity by a method similar to that at the Ajanta and Ellora caves where, to show the sequence of events, principal figures are repeated in different poses and surroundings in a continuous narrative. Vishnu Ananta Shayin, the primordial godhead, is first shown sleeping on the snake of eternity. Then, having risen out of the cosmic ocean, he is again depicted standing majestically in all his glory, supported by his lovely consort Lakshmi and two Nagas. The dramatic effect is enhanced by the numerous gods and goddesses, Apsarases and Gandharvas, which surround Vishnu, offering their homage. Their well-shaped limbs, hair styles, jewellery, sophisticated elegance and marvellously balanced, harmonious and rhythmic gestures represent all that is finest and noblest in the Gupta style at its peak. In sheer sculptural quality and sensitive handling of the subject, the Nepalese sculptors have clearly excelled the craftsmen of Deogarh.

Remarkable among the individual figures is **The Buddha** (page 181). This figure, still half buried on the banks of the Bhagmati river near the Pashupatinath temple, is comparable to some of the greatest master-

pieces of 5th Century AD Sarnath sculpture and illustrates the final realisation of the Gupta style. The smooth transparent robe completely revealing the lovely swelling fullness of the warmth of the flesh beneath is of a crystalline perfection. The exquisitely modelled and peaceful face also displays to extraordinary perfection sweeping lines, simplicity and immaculate purity. It is difficult to improve upon this description by Benjamin Rowland, Jr. of a 5th Century AD Sarnath head of the Buddha, which exactly pins down the qualities of the godhead. "The type represents the ultimate refinement of precedents of the Gandhara Kushan schools. It is the final Indian ideal for the Buddha face. Under the brows curved like a bow, the lotus-petal eyes are engraved in low relief. The full, flower-like lips repeat their gentle curves. All of these features are completely integrated within the mass of the head and the perfect ovoid of its contour. As in all masterpieces of the Gupta period, there is an almost geometric perfection of form in the uninterrupted smoothness of the facial planes and, at the same time, by its description in quiet circular shapes, the face radiates a feeling of infinite serenity and purity."

The "infinite serenity and purity" of the Buddha's face is of comparable merit with a lovely face of Parvati carved on **Shivalinga** (page 175). The piece is on the left bank of river Bhagmati on the outskirts of the Pashupatinath temple area, and like the Buddha (page 181) it is half buried in the ground. This remarkable head of Parvati (Shiva's consort) with its neat hair style and its expression of meditation radiating from a blissful face with closed eyes, is typical of the Gupta style. The piece as a whole is certainly among the finest of the numerous Shivalingas in the Nepal valley, partly because of the perfect balance of the proportions of the Lingam itself and the mass of the Parvati's head which is carved on the phallus.

Similar dazzling brilliance of expression is convincingly displayed by the sculpture **A Noble Man** (page 185). The figure is on the right bank of the river Bhagmati, near the Pashupatinath temple, and it was photographed while the waters of the river in spate were splashing up to its hips. While conforming to all the basic precepts of classical construction by which the figure of the Buddha (page 181) is made, the sculptor has succeeded in drawing an invisible but incredibly clear line of division between the secular and the religious. Its powerful simplicity is primarily due to its concise, well-proportioned and balanced outlines. The effectiveness of this technique is enhanced by doing away with the traditional symbols and gestures, ornaments and elaborate garments, and simplifying the Gupta-style hair curls as compared to the ones seen in the Vishnu Vishvarupa frieze.

Nepal's cultural contacts with the western parts of India were not interrupted with the rise to power of the Thakuri dynasty under Amshuvarman (593—621 AD), a Rajput prince. Probably he belonged to the Maukharis, the restless aggressive tribal leaders along the Rajast-

SHIVALINGA, PASHUPATINATH TEMPLE, NEPAL. 6th CENTURY AD.

VISHNU VISHVARUPA, CHANGU NARAYAN, NEPAL. 5th—6th CENTURY AD.

han desert, who in the 6th Century were continually trying to gain access to the rich agricultural lands towards the east and the Himalaya. Amshuvarman's family had risen to power in India under Ishanavarman of Kanauj (*c.* 554 AD) and were relatives of the great Harshavardhana of Thanesar. He had married the daughter of king Vishvadeva and assisted his father-in-law until he himself assumed power. This was an exciting period in the histories of Nepal, India and Tibet, as Amshuvarman was a contemporary of Harshavardhana of India and Srongtsengampo of Tibet. To consolidate his power in Nepal, Amshuvarman entered into a matrimonial alliance with Tibet by giving the hand of his daughter, Bhrikuti, to the Tibetan king. Tradition has it that a

A VIEW OF THE PASHUPATINATH TEMPLE AND THE RIVER BHAGMATI, NEPAL.

sandalwood image of the Buddha carried by the princess as a wedding present to Srongtsen-gampo consolidated Buddhism in Tibet. Bhrikuti herself was deified as the "Harit Tara" (green Tara), while the king's second wife, a Chinese T'ang princess, was venerated as the "Sweta Tara" (white Tara). Images of these goddesses are still seen in monasteries throughout the Himalaya.

Towards the south, Harshavardhana, a grandson of a Gupta princess, revived imperial memories of Samudragupta by showing a considerable taste for literature and arts that brings to mind the versatile hero of Harishena's panegyric. The cultural intercourse between Nepal and India during this period was noted by the famous Chinese pilgrim, Hsuan Tsang, who in his memoirs (643 AD) of Harshavardhana's kingdom did not forget to mention the art of Nepal, even if he did not himself visit that country. "The people of Nepal", he wrote, "among other things are skilled in arts. Their houses are made of wood and carved."

During Amshuvarman's reign some iconographical influences from eastern India had already begun to creep into the prevalent predominantly western style. This is shown by the eight arms of **Bachhaleshvari** (page 207). It is an interesting piece displaying an important link with the development of the cult of the Mother Goddess in eastern India, while at the same time retaining its connection with the western art schools. The latter influence is shown not only by the Gupta style but also by the Kushan type of umbrella under which the goddess is seated. Moreover, while the outlines are drawn according to the rules applied by the Gupta precepts, the elegance of the high Gupta style has given way to rather more voluminous figures that display ponderous attitudes. It is a beautiful work of art, nevertheless, in which, despite the difficult introduction of new iconographical elements such as the eight arms, the craftsmen have achieved a perfect balance of composition.

Nepal's intimate cultural contacts with India were continued during the post-Amshuvarman period. In 672 AD, the most powerful scion of the later Gupta period in the Ganges valley was Adityasena who had strengthened his position by matrimonial alliances with the most illustrious royal families of his age. His granddaughter became the queen of Shivadeva II of Nepal (680—705 AD) and mother of his successor king Jayadeva II (705—740 AD). At this period the Gupta style experienced a far-reaching transformation as sculptures began to take on massive proportions. This tendency was accelerated by the enthusiasm of the Rashtrakuta governors in India who enjoyed a considerable autonomy in the northern provinces of the empire. A grandiose art devoted to the great Hindu gods resulted in the massive monolithic sculptures which can be seen in the cave temples dedicated to Shiva at Ellora and at Elephanta and Mandapeshvar, near Bombay. In a similar development in Nepal, **Ananta Shayin Narayana** (page 196) was also conceived on a mighty scale. This sculpture of Vishnu (over

SHIVA AND PARVATI, PATAN, NEPAL, LATE PERIOD.

five meters long) lies in a tank fed by the waters of a natural spring at Buddhanilakantha. It was dedicated by the ruler Bhimarjuna Deva and his regent Vishnugupta; an inscription also mentions that it was built by "Koli" people who were amply rewarded by the patrons. This massive work of art, in which Vishnu Narayana is shown sleeping on a bed made by the coils of the serpent Ananta, creates an atmosphere of superhuman serenity and profound peace. On closer examination, however, the image does not compare well with the Vishnu Vishvarupa frieze at Changu Narayan, though it is a replica on a grand scale of that part of the frieze in which Vishnu is depicted resting on the serpent. All the motifs, such as the crown, garments, ornaments, symbols and even the pose in which Vishnu lies with his feet crossed are identical in both cases. The only difference is in the carving of the hood of the serpent showing one more fang than the seven in the Changu Narayan

A ROYAL PERSONAGE, NEPAL. *c.* 4th CENTURY AD.

sculpture. Yet, the piece is indicative of a declining style which by its ambitious anxiety to surpass its model by inflating the dimensions has, in fact, defeated its very purpose.

The tendency at this time towards making large images appears to have been common in many parts of the Himalaya. The brass idols of Brahmor and Chatrarhi, an offshoot of the late Gupta style, were also made in sizes of over one meter—unusually big for metal images. As pointed out by H. Goetz, "Decisive Gupta influence is apparent in 7th Century Nepal, indeed to such a degree that it has left its mark on the whole later development of Nepalese art. The amazing aesthetic affinity between the art of Brahmor kingdom (now Himachal Pradesh) and Nepalese art is due not to any interrelations, but to a common dependence on the Gupta style in the age of Harshavardhana".

Towards the end of the 8th Century AD, an expedition of king Jayapida of Kashmir into the Himalayan region of Nepal was repelled by king Aramundi, and can be regarded as symbolic also of the end of the influences from the west. When Nepal emerged from the political upheavals of the post-Amshuvarman period, its art from the 9th to the 12th Centuries AD was totally inspired by the great centres of the Pala kingdom of Bengal-Bihar in north-east India. Taking advantage of the disappearance of the later Guptas from the Indian political scene and the chaos following the collapse of Lalitaditya's Kashmiri empire, the people of eastern Bengal had installed Gopala as their king. Dharmapala (*c*. 770—815 AD) and Devapala (*c*. 815—54 AD) expanded the Pala territories until checked by the Partiharas of Rajasthan and Rasthtrakutas of the Deccan. After a decline in the 9th and 10th Centuries, the Pala kingdom rose once again, reaching the peak of its glory under Mahipala (*c*. 922—1040 AD) and Ramapala (1084—1126 AD). Subsequently, the Palas were replaced by their vassals, the Senas (*c*. 1150—1280 AD) who were originally Brahman immigrants from the Deccan. Their most outstanding king was Lakshmanasena, a great patron of the arts, who was eventually ousted from his capital by the Muslims in 1206 AD.

The rule of the Thakuri and early Malla dynasties of Nepal coincides with the medieval period of Indian art when Pala art was supreme. The Pala style in Nepal, evolving from Gupta standards, was naturally affected by regional talents and local religious and cult affiliations, although stylistically the transitional period was almost identical to the development from declining Gupta classicism towards the style of the Palas. In the 8th Century, the output of this school of Bihar and Bengal was already prolific and partly for that reason the style lacked ingenuity, perhaps because the craftsmen thoughtlessly imitated the Gupta formulae. As the sculptors followed iconographic rules very strictly, the art lost much of its creative impetus and, in the process, the free standing images became rather heavy and lost their former vigour, even though they are larger and very close to the Gupta style. An example of this is **Lakshmi** (page 189). The shape of the crown with

THE BUDDHA, PASHUPATINATH TEMPLE, NEPAL. 5th—6th CENTURY AD.

UMASAHITA-MAHESHVARA, PATAN, NEPAL. 10th CENTURY AD.

VARAHA, DHUM VARAHI, NEPAL, 5th CENTURY AD.

round pendants is similar to the one worn by Vishnu Vishvarupa, but the flower designs have become more elaborate. The transparency of the garments, which was indicated by simple incised lines on the 5th—6th Century AD sculptures, continues to be shown by a similar technique, but it is now more intricate. The craftsmen's attempt to produce a calm, peaceful atmosphere by making the goddess stand firmly on her two feet has, on the contrary, resulted in a nervous tension, displaying a visionary mysticism behind the outward show of superhuman energy. Heavy voluminous bodies are also characteristic of this style before it gave way to the sophisticated elegance of the later Pala period.

The tortoise on which Lakshmi stands is not a part of the same sculpture, but appears to belong to a later period. It is an interesting piece, nevertheless. Kurma, or the tortoise, is the form in which Vishnu appeared in the Satya Yuga, or first age, to recover valuable things that had been lost in the deluge. He converted himself into a tortoise and, placing himself at the bottom of the sea of milk, he used the mountain Mandara as a pivot. The gods and demons twisted the great serpent Vasuki round the mountain, and churned the sea until they recovered the desired objects. Among the finds was Lakshmi, the goddess of fortune and beauty, and consort of Vishnu.

In time, with greater specialisation, several of the qualities of Gupta art, such as its subtle sensuality and its vivid appreciation of form and pattern, once again began to emerge. At first this new intensity of life was infused more by proliferation of figures in limited spaces, than by any indication of movement of limb or gestures. An example of this is the **Heavenly Court of Vishnu** (page 191). This surviving right-hand panel of the frieze from the Pashupatinath temple is carved out of bluish-black stone by the expert hands of Nepalese craftsmen. It makes use of the Gupta method of interpreting the theme as a kind of theatrical representation and so creates a scene seething with the typical Gupta style elephant profiles, creatures such as Makaras, a crowd of deities and attendants, etc. But unlike the Gupta representations, the panel as a whole conveys a feeling of a pattern rather than action. The Gupta conventions and clichés are still intact, even to such details as the uniform of the Gupta soldiers, whose jackets were made of interwoven metal plates. (An identical figure clad in uniform with a similar bow and arrow is seen in the far right-hand edge of the Vishnu Vishvarupa frieze.) It is, nevertheless, a definite stylistic advance from the earlier period, as the figures have discarded their irksome heaviness and display their slender but erect and powerful bodies. The expertly carved figures, though a bit self-conscious, distinctly stand out of the "pattern", like the Nepalese music in which the repetition of the beat is merely the background and not the focus of attention.

The forms of Pala bronzes produced in Nalanda and Kurkihar in Bihar during the 8th and 9th Centuries greatly influenced the stone sculptures

VISHNU, PATAN, NEPAL, LATE PERIOD.

of Nepal. The figures came to wear the triple pointed crown and the drapery became more elaborate, with the ends folded into a conical shape and falling between the legs. The Prabhavali or enclosing frame was decorated with more elaborate floral designs and rounded on the top. The figures also became more elegant though not elongated as in the subsequent period.

In 879 AD, when king Raghavadeva ushered in a new era called the Nepal Samvat, a slight shift seems to have taken place also in the cult affiliations of the Nepalese people and artists. Vishnu, who had been for centuries in the centre of the stage, now began to share this honour on equal level with Shiva. Many images of Shiva's family, called Uma-sahita-Maheshvara, found in the Nepal valley from this period were

THE BUDDHA, SVAYAMBHUNATH TEMPLE, NEPAL. 9th—10th CENTURY AD.

LAKSHMI, PASHUPATINATH TEMPLE, NEPAL. 8th CENTURY AD.

*NATIVITY
OF THE BUDDHA.*
KATHMANDU, NEPA
LATE
10th CENTURY AD.

*HEAVENLY COURT
OF VISHNU,*
PASHUPATINATH
TEMPLE, NEPAL.
EARLY
9th CENTURY AD.

made continuously for over 400 years. The earliest dated known image of Umasahita-Maheshvara (1012 AD) is at Patan and belongs to the time of Bhojadeva-Rudradeva, while another inscribed piece of the time of Gunakamadeva is dated 1186 AD. Judging from the variations in style between these two dated sculptures, the undated **Umasahita-Maheshvara** (page 183) reproduced here appears to be earlier and may be placed in the 10th Century. As in all such groups, in this frieze the lord of the mountain is shown, with his bull Nandi, enthroned on Mount Kailasha with his consort Uma, "the light". At the top, the river Ganges is seen in the background emerging from the crevasses in the rocks, flanked by the deities representing the sun and the moon. Below the throne where the divine couple sit are the Ganas, or Shiva's attendants, whose commander is the elephant-headed Ganesha. According to mythology, the Ganas also dwell on Kailasha and are minor deities who are invariably depicted in groups. In this beautiful sculpture Shiva and his consort, with their poise and balance in repose, are a most striking portrayal of blissful union. The slightly smiling, calm and serene face of Shiva with almost closed eyes radiates majesty, while he places his principal left hand on the right shoulder of the goddess. The youthful divinities are attentive to each other, yet soothingly relaxed, as shown by the sculptor's masterly handling of Uma's posture. The weight of her half-reclining, elegant and slim figure is carried by her right arm which is placed on Shiva's left thigh. Both the figures are robust but well-shaped, the ornaments and garments tasteful and the composition well-balanced, showing a remarkable advance of sculptural proficiency over earlier pieces depicting similar themes, such as the Heavenly Court of Vishnu (page 191).

In the beginning of the 10th Century AD the tendency towards elongation of forms which in Bengal and Bihar was carried to its logical extreme during the Sena period also became popular in Nepal. The Nepalese figures, however, retain a much better sense of proportion due to their sculptor's complete mastery and control of the techniques of cutting the hard stone. This quality in seen in **Nativity of the Buddha** (page 190). This limestone sculpture shows a scene at Lumbini where Gautama Buddha was born. The tall figure of his mother, Maya Devi, is seen elegantly supporting herself on the equally flexible branch of a tree. Resting her weight on one foot she stands with her feet crossed so that her arched hips form a Tribhanga or the pose of three bends. Her tapering, beautiful hands are clasped together holding a bunch of flowers without interrupting the easy flow of her arms. The soft, slender figure, narrow waist and well-shaped round breasts are all reminiscent of the late Gupta style paintings such as the dancing girl with musicians in cave I of Ajanta. Her simple ornaments comprise a diadem over the forehead, Kundalas (ear ornaments), two necklaces, armlets, a triple-stranded waist band and plain Nupuras (anklets). The newly-born infant Buddha is seen standing upright on a double lotus pedestal against an oval nimbus. Two celestial figures in heaven are shown among stylised clouds, raining holy water and lotuses. The sculptor of this relief has successfully produced a spectacular scene; and yet that inner thrill of wonder and religious fervour which Vishnu Vikrantamurti (page 169) or Vishvarupa (page 175) convey are conspicuously lacking, possibly because of the rather affected movements of Maya Devi's figure.

The sharp variations sometimes noticed in the style of depicting Hindu deities and the minor deities of Buddhist legends, such as Maya Devi, are almost completely absent in the making of images of Buddha himself. For fear of blasphemy, the sacrosanct figures of the Buddha strictly adhere to the precepts laid down by the treatises of the Gupta period; the only slight modifications being in the floral motifs outlining the Prabhavali and in certain regional variations in the facial features which crept in unconsciously. A lovely example of a life-size Buddha in the Pala style can be seen in the courtyard of the Svayambhunath temple. **The Buddha** (page 188) is done in a style which is the final development of the Buddhist art of making the image of the master, perfected in the famous monasteries of Bodh Gaya, Nalanda and later Vikramashila in the Ganges plain. The stele shows the Buddha carved with the body bent in a gentle curve—a manner which is typical of countless figures. The style is essentially a repetition of the ideal Gupta figures in which the pose was sculptured in such a way as to suggest by a feeling of movement that the Buddha was approaching the devotee. As usual in Pala sculpture, it also reflects the Gupta canon in a dry, precise technique, although this wonderfully proportioned statue still retains something of the freshness of feeling produced by the immaculate soft surface and warm sense of volume. Like the 5th Century AD Sarnath Buddhas, the figure is formed with a feeling of sinuous linear rhythms and has exquisite precision of craftsmanship.

By the beginning of the 11th Century, the later Gupta mannerism seems to have been completely superseded by the Pala style. Very many bronzes of excellent workmanship in gold and silver have been discovered at Nalanda, Kurkihar, Jhiwari (Chittagong) and Rangpur. These were the models which were interpreted and multiplied by Nepalese craftsmen to meet the ever-increasing demand of the Tibetan Buddhists, as they came to India and Nepal to visit the holy places of Buddhist legends. After the despoiling of the great Buddhist monasteries in the Ganges plain by the Muslim iconoclasts in the middle of the 13th Century AD, the Nepalese centres of art production took over the role of exporting religious icons to Tibetan monasteries and temples. These art centres flourished under a new dynasty which came to power in the Nepal valley in about 1200 AD beginning with the rule of Arimalla (1200—16 AD). The Mallas claimed descent from the ancient Mallas of Pawa and Kusinara, who were contemporaries of Buddha and are mentioned in Buddhist literature. Mallas were also known in the great

ANANTA SHAYIN NARAYANA, BUDDHA NILAKANTHA, NEPAL.
LATE 7th CENTURY AD.

Indian epic *Mahabharata*. In Nepal they were mentioned for the first time in a Changu Narayan inscription by Manadeva dated 464 AD.

The importance of the Nepalese art centres under the Malla dynasty is shown by the fact that Nepalese artists enjoyed great fame in Tibet. The renown of the Nepalese craftsmen was such that when Kublai Khan asked his spiritual leader, the Sakya-abbot Pags-pa, to erect a golden stupa in Tibet, the Abbot could not think of better craftsmen than the Nepalese. Jayabhima Deva, the ruler of Nepal at that time, chose a young relation of his, Balbahu (1245—1306 AD), whom the Tibetans and Chinese call Aniko, to lead a contingent of eighteen talented Nepalese craftsmen. Despite his youth, Balbahu was already an accomplished bronze-caster when he went to Tibet. He carried out his mission so successfully that Pags-pa persuaded him to go to China, where he entered the service of Kublai Khan. In 1274 AD, he became the chief of all bronze workers and by 1278 AD was appointed the controller of imperial manufacturers.

Unfortunately, in Nepal it is difficult these days to find really outstanding early bronzes, particularly of Hindu deities. An exceptional piece is **Madhava** (pages 224-25), which is another name of Vishnu. Stylistically, this bronze can be placed very accurately between the barefooted standing figure of Surya in limestone which is dated 1030 AD, and another similarly standing image of Vishnu, also in limestone, on which the date 1417 AD is inscribed. Both these pieces are in the Kathmandu Museum. The style of the crown, the ornaments, the garments and the erect posture of the standing figure of Madhava is almost an identical replica of the Surya, except for the slightly thickset limbs which give an illusion of a short-statured body. This latter peculiarity was amplified in the 15th Century AD figures which progressively become stocky and short. The drapery whose ends are folded into a conical shape and lowered centrally between the legs also appears to be popular in the early period and subsequently either completely disappeared as in Vishnu (1417 AD), or is considerably shortened, as in **Padmapani Lokeshvara** (page 201). Padmapani Lokeshvara is a large bronze, over a meter in height, now placed in one of the corners of the Hiranyavarna Mahavihara courtyard in Kwathabahal at Patan. The Buddhist deity is conventionally depicted in Nepal with one head and two arms; the right hand displaying the Varadha Mudra, or boon-bestowing gesture, and the other holding the stem of a lotus (which in this case has fallen off). As is evident, this 17th Century AD bronze is of doubtful merit, having lost many of those qualities which made the Nepalese bronzes among the finest in the world.

At Changu Narayan (where the masterpieces of Vishnu Vishvarupa lies) there are also some very outstanding stone sculptures from the 12th and 13th Centuries AD. In addition to some of the qualities and peculiarities of the Pala and Sena styles, these pieces display a special stylistic element termed "ornateness" which was characteristic of

SUMBHA AND NISUMBHA, TALEJU BHAVANI TEMPLE, BHATGAON, NEPAL.
17th CENTURY AD.

medieval sculptures in the Karnataka region in southern India. This consciously decorative style is considered to have been introduced to Nepal, during the short-lived influence in the Terai region of Nepal, of Nanyadeva, who is believed to have hailed from the Karnataka region. Nanyadeva's capital was Simraongarh in the Terai and his influence in the Nepal valley lasted for about 150 years from 1097—1245 AD. Basing his derivations from several inscriptions such as those of Someshvara I Vhalukya of Kalyan (1047 AD) and Kalachuri Bijjala (1200 AD), L. Petech states that "Some kind of a religious and cultural influence did penetrate from the south of India at this time".

An element of ornateness is clearly discernible in **Vaikunthanatha**

DEVI BHAVANI, TALEJU BHAVANI TEMPLE, BHATGAON, NEPAL. 17th CENTURY AD.

(page 211). The floral background against which the majestic figure of
lord Vishnu is carved and the symmetrically spreading hands and
wings of the sun-eagle Garuda on which Vishnu is seated, recall some
of the sculptures of the Chalukyas and Kalachuris. But this element of
ornateness has hardly distracted the sculptors at all from evoking the
imagery of Vishnu's glory in heaven and entirely focussing the attention
of the devotee on the lord of paradise. Unlike the highly stylised
carvings of south India with predominating ornamentation, elaborate
jewellery and crowns, scrolls, flowers, trees as background, all of them
done in a fine filigree work in which the rather expressionless figures
of gods and goddesses are completely lost, the Vaikunthanatha frieze

199

exhibits a marvellous sense of discrimination. Here, the ornateness is effectively used to project the principal aim—to keep Vishnu in the centre of the stage—while everything else is subordinated and overshadowed by his radiating personality and majesty. This marvellous sculpture, in which the heavenly throne of Vaikunthanatha is formed by the outstretched arms and wings of his vehicle Garuda, projects a wonderful feeling of lightness, as the sun-eagle appears about to take off. This effect is accentuated by the fine polished surface of the hard and heavy stone from which the figures are carved, and the rhythmical composition conveys a feeling of movement in serene stillness.

In similar style but in complete contrast with the peaceful atmosphere of Vaikunthanatha, is the beautiful frieze **Narasimha Avatara** (page 171). Vibrating with action, this violent scene is a convincing testimony of the ability, capacity and competence of the Nepalese craftsmen who could twist and turn the brittle, hard stone into incredible shapes. Here, Vishnu is depicted in the man-animal form of Narasimha, which he assumed to deliver the world from the tyranny of Hiranyakasipu. The demon had become invulnerable by favour of Brahma, so that no god, man or animal could kill him. According to the legend, Hiranyakasipu tried to kill his own son, Prahlada, because the latter was a devotee of Vishnu. In the course of an argument over the omnipotence and omnipresence of Vishnu, the demon, demanding to know if Vishnu was present in a stone pillar of the royal courtyard, struck it violently. To avenge his devotee, Vishnu came forth from the pillar as neither god, nor man, nor animal, but as half-man, half-lion, and tore the arrogant demon king to pieces.

The Vaikunthanatha and Narasimha Avatara sculptures are the final flowering of a style which is unministakably Nepalese. It is the result of centuries of intelligent study and practice by which the finest elements of all the styles that had gone before were discriminately selected and assimilated. The style of the lion on the capitals of Ashoka's columns, the homely folk art style of the Sungas, the strength and vigour of Mathura Yoga postures, the measured, harmonious movements of the classical Gupta figures and, lastly, the slender but powerful bodies of the late Pala sculptures, finally produced a completely original synthesis in the style of Nepal. To quote D. R. Regmi, "The old Nepalese style of art inspired by the Eastern school, known as the Pala school, continued to influence the iconography. But in detail there were deviations from the strict observance of the canons of Pala art tending to create varieties. There might also be fluctuations in the standard of achievement. But the continuity of the tradition was maintained and their essentials did not alter; in fact, a distinction can be made only in point of detail. But details are sometimes dominant enough to impart such characteristics to the image which make them a distinct category by themselves".

Painting in Nepal, like sculpture, also progressed under identical stylist

PADMAPANI LOKESHVARA, HIRANYAVARNA MAHAVIHARA, PATAN. 17th CENTURY AD.

influences. Traditionally, Chitrabhasa, or painting, was regarded as a king of solid representation; a monk "raises" a picture (Vinaya), or a painter "raises up" a shape on a wall surface by means of his brush and colours (Samyutta Nikaya). This was inevitable, as the art of painting evidently came into its own during the phase of development when sculpture in the round declined, and the reliefs on the railings and walls of early Buddhist monuments began to be covered with layers of bright colours to enliven the stone's dull surface. Subsequently, the rules for sculpture became valid for painting. With the passage of time the influence of relief on painting gradually decreased as examples began to be carried from place to place in the form of paintings on rolled canvases (called Patas or Paubhas in Nepal). Both *Ashokavadana* and *Harshacharita* mention the travelling story-tellers who, to illustrate the glories of a god, displayed these paintings on two bamboo poles held in their left hand, pointing out the legends with a reed in their right hand. In the Buddhist monasteries in the Himalaya, too, art prototypes were first brought on these Patas and through the medium of illustrated manuscripts, the oldest of which date only from the Pala period. The manuscripts were written and painted on long, narrow palm leaves, as paper was introduced in India only about the 12th Century AD. The earliest known example of the small illustrations of Buddhist figures on palm leaves and on wooden book covers, which brought the Pala style to Nepal is dated 1028 AD. Such paintings reveal, as A. K. Coomaraswamy has stated, "A hieratic style like the Pala and Gujarati schools in the 11th century. The distinction of style as between the Bengali and Nepali illustrated manuscripts is so slight as to be scarcely definable in a few words". This style, while preserving the characteristics of Buddhist paintings, notably the sensuous elegance and refinement of the Ajanta manner, became flat in the later period. Like the Pala school of painting in Bengal, the effectiveness of their conception rested entirely on linear emphasis in which flat, glittering colours were meticulously filled in. This tradition in sytle was reinforced in the wake of the Muslim conquests of Bengal in the 12th and 13th Centuries AD, when some of the scholars and craftsmen from Nalanda and Vikramashila took refuge in the Nepal valley.

This influx was responsible to a great degree for introducing Tantric influences from Bengal in the form that became very popular in Nepal during the 14th Century AD. The word "Tantra" is actually mentioned in the Gangadhar inscription of the year 423 AD; but the Tantric cults did not come out into the open until the 7th Century AD when they gave rise to the concept of Shakti Pithas. This was associated with the cult of Shakti, or the mother goddess. The concept of Matrikas (divine mothers) was not new. These were the seven or eight female energies of the great gods, Brahmani of Brahma, Maheshvari of Shiva, Vaishnavi of Vishnu, etc. From these evolved the idea of 64 Yoginis with their 64 Bhaiaravas, or forms of Shiva in their terrifying aspect. In this ever-

202   *DANCING VISHNU*, TALEJU BHAVANI TEMPLE, NEPAL. 17th CENTURY AD.

SARANGIKA AND JARITA, TALEIU BHAVANI TEMPLE, NEPAL. 17th CENTURY AD.

GANAPATIHARDAYA, TALEJU BHAVANI TEMPLE, NEPAL. 17th CENTURY AD.

A LOKAPALA ELEPHANT, TALEJU BHAVANI TEMPLE, NEPAL. 17th CENTURY AD.

UNNATI, TALEJU BHAVANI TEMPLE, NEPAL. 17th CENTURY AD.

expanding pantheon, the Mahadevi (great goddess), the consort of the principal aspect of Shiva, became the supreme object of devotion in Nepal during the Malla period. She owes her great distinction to the *Markandeya Purana*—in which there is an episode of 700 verses called *Chandi Mahatmaya*—and to later works such as the *Devi Bhagavatam*, scriptures celebrating the Devi's victories over the demons.

As Shakti, or the female energy of Shiva, Devi is a perfect symbol of Indian esotericism which taught that her fierce character is simply the belligerent aspect of her tranquil forces, which appear from time to time to conquer their evil counterparts. In her milder form, she is the beautiful Uma (light), Gauri (yellow or brilliant), Parvati (the mountaineer); on the other hand, as Kali (black,) Chandika (fierce) and Bhairavi (terrible) she is respectively represented with a black complexion, a terrible and hideous countenance and wearing necklaces of human skulls dripping with blood. In Nepal she is also named Taleju and one of the several interesting temples dedicated to her is at Bhatgaon.

Taleju appears to have established herself in the valley about the time of the sack of Kathmandu, Bhatgaon and Patan at the hands of Shamsuddin Ilyas of Bengal in 1349 AD, a disaster which brought about a devotional and iconographic transformation similar to that which had

204

A MYTHICAL CREATURE,
TALEJU BHAVANI TEMPLE, NEPAL.
17th CENTURY AD.

KARKOT NAGA AND HIS CONSORT,
TALEJU BHAVANI TEMPLE, NEPAL.
17th CENTURY AD.

BHAIRAVA,
TALEJU BHAVANI TEMPLE,
NEPAL. 17th CENTURY AD.

resulted from the Hun attacks against the Gupta empire. At that time, as now, emphasis began to be placed on the fierce aspect of the gods and goddesses. The *Vamshavalis*, however, give this credit to Raja Harisimha Deva, who is said to have fled to Nepal to save himself from the Muslims. Harisimha Deva's presence in Nepal has not been confirmed and historians are divided in their opinions on the subject. The *Vamshavali* narrative is, nevertheless, interesting as an instance of the interconnection between fact and fiction, religion and mythology, in the Himalayan region of which the wall-paintings of the Taleju Bhavani temple at Bhatgaon are a true reflection. It is stated in the *Vamshavalis* that "The Raja Harisimha Deva, a descendant of Ramachandra, being hard-pressed by the Muslim invaders, fled to Simraongarh. His wife had a Keti, a slave girl, whose paramour was a Rakshasa, a demon from Ceylon, called Mayabija, who as a renowned architect. One night when the slave girl was sweeping the floor of the palace with a golden broom given to her by her lover, the Raja apprehended the Rakshasa and ordered him to build a temple to his household goddess Turja Bhavani. Mayabija accordingly erected in one night a five-storied temple with beautiful images of gods and goddesses, tanks full of clear water containing red lotuses, surrounded by gardens full of flowers and singing birds which rivalled in beauty the Nandana-bana of Indra in heaven. For the protection of the temple he built a wall round the city so high and formidable that neither beasts nor enemies could scale it. However, the cock crew at dawn before the works was completed and he was obliged to stop, leaving a portion of the wall unfinished. As a result, when Simraongarh was attacked by a large army of invaders, they succeeded in taking the city by entering the portion of the wall which had been left unfinished by Mayabija. The Raja escaped and on Turja Bhavani's directions he went to Bhatgaon in Nepal. Thus the people of Bhatgaon came to see the goddess, and such was her influence that he, without much ado, made over the kingdom to Harisimha Deva. He established the goddess there in a temple which he named Mula Chowk."

The reign of Jayasthiti Malla (1382—95 AD) marks a period of social recovery in Nepal; an improvement which was maintained by his equally talented and capable son, Jyotir Malla (1408—28 AD) and grandson, Yaksha Malla (1428—82 AD). Some of the paintings in the Taleu Bhavani temple appear to have been done under the patronage of these rulers. Carved along the wall facing north of the main square, there is a rectangular gallery, 12 by 25 meters, the interior of which is painted with miniature paintings (between 12 and 25 centimeters in height) in three rows, one above the other, and barely a meter above the ground. This gallery appears to be the original Thara (a kind of parapet) of the palace, and judging from the size and style of the paintings they are certainly the earliest. There was already a flourishing school of paintings in western Tibet in this style which was born of imitation, first of Kashmiri, then of Bengali and Nepalese art. Biographies of the most famous founder abbots mention Nepalese painters who were commissioned to paint the walls of newly built shrines. In some cases actual names of Nepalese artists are recorded, as at the chapel built by the founder of the Ngor Sect, Kuinga-Sangpo (1382—1444 AD). An example of this style is **Sati** (page 24). Daughter of Daksha and wife of Shiva, Sati abandoned her body because of a quarrel between her father and her husband. According to the *Kashikhanda*, he burnt herself and became a Sati (figure on the left). She was then reborn as goddess Devi, daughter of Himalaya and Mena (figure on the right). The story resembles the Egyptian fable of Isis and Osiris.

The painting has faded considerably with time, but a very rich colour spectrum can still be seen. The method adopted in preparing the surface, drawing and colouring is, with slight variations, very similar to that adopted in the Ajanta caves at the beginning of the Christian era. The wall was first covered with two or three layers of slaked lime mixed with water and animal glue. The surface of the thickened and dried lime was then polished by rubbing it with a smooth substance. (Contrary to practice at Ajanta, in Nepal rice husk was not employed to increase the tenacity of the plaster.) The surface having been thus prepared, the figures were traced in black with soot from oil lamps, always beginning

BACHHALESHVARI, PASHUPATINATH TEMPLE, NEPAL. 7th CENTURY AD.

with the central figure as the nucleus round which the secondary scenes were then drawn. Paintings belonging to a later period also used black outlines, sometimes with Indian ink replacing the soot. The colours, mainly from mineral sources, were then filled in, prominent colours being red, yellow, vitriol green, carmine, indigo, lime white, and blue from lapis-lazuli.

The paintings in the rectangular gallery of the Mula Chowk are easily distinguishable (quite apart from their small size) from those of the later period in the main courtyard by their brightness and vivacity of colours and elegance of drawing. Though greatly effaced, the style of these paintings retains a nostalgic faint memory of the Ajanta sense of marvellous movement, perspective, balance and composition.

On Yaksha Malla's death in 1482 AD the valley was divided between his three quarrelsome sons into three small kingdoms, Kathmandu, Lalitpur (Patan) and Bhakatpur (Bhatgaon). The last named kingdom was assigned to his eldest son, Raya Malla. The family divisions and territorial jealousies among the otherwise talented and versatile successors of Yaksha Malla did not, however hinder the cultural renaissance in the valley. The Malla rulers of the divided kingdoms, in fact, vied with each other in building in their respective territories beautiful temples containing paintings and sculptures. They patronised poets, artists, musicians, and introduced dances and Rathyatras (religious chariot processions). Artists thus acquired a new prestige and an elevated status in the social hierarchy. A legend narrates that the absence of the painters of Bhatgaon from the religious bathing ceremony of Machhindra Natha resulted in a series of catastrophes, so that the holy chariot carrying the image "was stuck in the mud and could not reach its destination in time."

By the 16th Century, the Nepalese art of painting had become well-established. Like the sculptors in Balbahu's tradition, Nepalese painters were also in demand in remote areas deep in the mountainous regions of Tibet. Such was the popularity and prestige of the art of painting that merchants coming from India through Nepal were asked to bring pigments, especially carmine and indigo. This is stated in a passage in the autobiography of the famous Tibetan polygrapher, Taranatha, who tells us that these colours were required as a part of the duty to be paid as transit fees to the customs officials.

In the race for cultural and artistic supremacy, Raya Malla's successors were perhaps the most creative and undoubtedly the most productive patrons. The golden age, by which this period of Nepal's history is known, is to a great extent due to Jagatprakasha Malla (1644—73 AD). Between 1655 and 1667 AD he built several temples and also made many additions with a view to improving the imagery of the Taleju Bhavani temple courtyard. The creative fervour and intense artistic activity of this period is indicated by the presence in Tibet of Nepalese artists—Dsy, Bhan, Siddhi, Mangal, Jaisingh, Amarajit and others—who worked

SURYA AND AN APSARAS WITH OFFERINGS, PATAN, NEPAL, LATE PERIOD.

for the fifth Dalai Lama (1659 AD). Jagatprakasha Malla's son, Jitamitra Malla (1673—96 AD) and his grandson, Bhupatindra Malla (1696—1722 AD) upheld this tradition. Under the patronage of these three rulers, additional paintings were made in the Mula Chowk and Bhairava or Sadashiva Chowk, to celebrate the fantastic legends of Mahadevi's exploits and victories over the demons.

The style of these 17th-18th Century AD paintings is clearly different from that of the 15th Century AD works represented by Sati (page 24). The emphasis on ornamentation is now absolute and the conception completely flat and linear, becoming a replica on a slightly larger scale of the illustrated manuscripts and their painted wooden covers. The prevalence of red and orange as the background, subdivided into squares and frames or other shapes, and on which there is superimposed an uninterrupted depiction of legend, are reminiscent of metrical biographies. The composition has become conventional and the movement rigid and abrupt.

Devi Bhairavi (page 199) and the demons **Sumbha and Nisumbha** (page 198) depict the legend as related in the *Markandeya Purana*. According to the mythology, Sumbha and Nisumbha, who were previously devotees of Shiva, performed a severe penance for 13,000 years to obtain immortality. At the instance of Indra, the efforts of Kama (the god of love) to thwart their ambitions did not succeed as the demons overcame the sensual passions to which they had earlier succumbed. Ultimately, Shiva granted them the boon that "in riches and strength they would excel the gods". Armed with their newly acquired power, Sumbha and Nisumbha then waged war against the deities, who in despair appealed in vain to Brahma, Vishnu and Shiva. At last Shiva advised the demoralised gods to appeal to his consort Devi Bhairavi, who subsequently fought the demons and defeated their powerful commanders, Chanda and Munda, and finally killed Sumbha and Nisumbha.

In Nepal the terrible aspect of Bhairavi in angry mood is depicted by the face of a sow in the same way as Shiva's face as Bhairava is that of a boar.

In a similar style is painted the **Dancing Vishnu** (page 203). The images of Vishnu often resemble those of his incarnation, Krishna, who is characterised as gentle and joyous. Here, Vishnu is seen dancing and beating a drum accompanied by his consort Lakshmi. Krishna is playing his flute and Krishna's wife, Radha, is playing a pair of cymbals. In the lower right-hand corner, Vishnu's vehicle Garuda is shown holding in his beak a snake, his eternal enemy. The composition seems to have been done after Tantric Buddhist models in which four divinities are generally depicted in four corners, around the central principal deity, for example the four Buddha Shaktis around Vajaradhatvishvari.

Sarangika and Jarita (page 203) is a delightful sketch of an equally charming legend about a childless saint, Mandapala, who could not attain heaven despite his long perseverance in devotion and asceticism. He enquired the reason from Yama, the keeper of hell, who told him that all his devotion had failed because he had no Putra (son). Mandapala then assumed the form of a bird called Sarangika, married another bird, Jarita, and gained fours sons.

The half-human and half-bird configuration of Sarangika and Jarita is among the hundreds of such configurations between men, women, mammals, reptiles, and birds, which are observed in Tantric art of this period. The three recurring configurations of man-animal, women-tree (Shalabhanjika) and the man-woman (Mithuna) were greatly expanded, creating some incredibly fantastic forms and symbols.

Ganapatihardaya (page 204) is the Shakti of Ganapati, the Tantric Buddhist counterpart of the Hindu elephant Ganesha. As a god of wisdom and remover of obstacles, this deity is universally popular. In this rather unusual painting the dancing figure of the woman-elephant

VAIKUNTHNATHA, CHANGU NARAYAN, NEPAL. 12th—13th CENTURY AD.

A *MANIFESTATION OF VISHNU*, KATHMANDU, NEPAL. 16th—17th CENTURY AD.

is shown in a charming pose, holding a rosary in one hand and an axe in another, while with her two principal hands she displays the Vyakhyana mudra or the gesture of discourse.

A corollary to the human-elephant configuration is the Tantric interpretation of **A Lokapala Elephant** (page 204). There are eight deities called Lokapalas, who support the world from eight directions. These are also admitted by Vajrayana Buddhism as Dikapalas, namely, Indra, Agni, Yama, Surya, Varuna, Vayu, Kuvera and Soma. Each of these deities has an elephant as his vehicle. The Lokapala Elephant in this painting is a strange mixture of an elephant and a bird, having also the horns of a bull, the mane of a horse and ears drawn to resemble the fins of a fish.

Unnati (page 204) is the wife of Garuda, the mythical half-human half-bird, on which Vishnu rides. Unnati, like her husband, has a white face and golden skin with a brilliant lustre so that "the gods mistaking her for fire worshipped her". She, too, hates the serpents. In the style of this Unnati drawing is also **A Mythical Creature** (page 205) of Tantric significance which has not been identified.

Karkot Naga and his Consort (page 205) is especially interesting as, according to the traditional belief, all the wealth and power of Nepal is vested in the serpent Karkot. The legend narrates that when Bodhisattva Manjushri cut through the southern side of the Himalaya and drained the Nepal valley, all the fish and serpents were washed away. However, Manjushri persuaded Karkot Naga to remain in exchange for all the wealth and power of the valley. In this painting the serpent is seen with his consort Nagini enjoying in their union the wealth and power of Nepal. Representations of Naga gods in Nepal up to about the 12th Century AD were in human form, with cobras having three, five, seven and eight hoods, spread behind their heads. After this period, the Nagas were shown with their bodies ending in serpents' tails. This was similar to the Indian practice where a peculiar convention was followed by which, when the cobra had only three or five hoods, the tail was spotted, while Nagas with more hoods were covered with scales.

Bhairava (page 205) or Shiva in his terrible form is also among the popular manifestations of man-animal configuration. Here, Shiva is depicted with the head of a boar in a Tandava dancing pose and wears a necklace of skulls called a Mundamala. In one hand he holds a Kapala, a cup made of a scalp, while in the other hand he has a noose called a Pasha. His neck is blue from drinking deadly poison which, had he not done so, would have destroyed the world.

With the passage of time, wall-paintings progressively became larger. In the early 18th Century some huge paintings were done in the Sadashiva Chowk under the patronage of Bhupatindra Malla (1696-1722 AD). **Bhupatindra Malla** (page 221) is a portrait about two meters high. According to convention, he is shewn here kneeling in prayer with folded hands, facing an even larger deity.

Basically, the style of these large-size paintings is, as before, an imitation of the miniature models on an extended area of the walls. Nevertheless, as broader spaces now required bigger brushes, the new element thus introduced brought about a significant modification of style. The outlines became more fluent, the colours plainer and the design bolder and more expressive. The extension of the linear element and the broad bands of colour necessitated also a certain degree of blending of the shaded areas to give an illusion of depth, even though there is no attempt at a three-dimensional perspective. This effect in modelling was

GANESHA, KATHMANDU, NEPAL. 16th—17th CENTURY AD.

MANASA, KATHMANDU, NEPAL. 18th CENTURY AD.

heightened, as in paintings in the Punjab Hill states, by juxtaposition of figures, making use of their sizes. This beautiful portrait is reminiscent of some of the quattrocento paintings in Italy.

An exquisite work of art of this period is the **door facade** in gilt, copper and brass of the Taleju temple in the palace at Bhatgaon (pages 192—3). It is said to be the earliest of its kind in Nepal and was made in the early 17th Century AD, although additions were successively made by Naresh Malla, Jagatprakasha Malla, Jitamitra Malla and Bhupatindra Malla. The doorway has a beautiful tympanum flanked by the images of Shari, standing on a Makara, and Lakshmi, whose vehicle is a tortoise. Shari and Lakshmi are described in early Vedic times as the two wives of Varuna. Varuna was the oldest of the six or seven celestial deities, Adityas, and enjoyed a supreme position as the maker and upholder of heaven and earth. Later, when Vishnu became the king of gods and universe, Shari and Lakshmi were identified as the same goddess and Vishnu's consort. Her images, however, continued to be in this dual character. The style of these figures and also the goddess Taleju in the centre of the tympanum above the door, surrounded by eight other emanations and enclosed by an arch formed by Garuda, is typical of this period. They display a very full modelling of the flesh and almost florid features. The noses are aquiline, but the lips are fully modelled. The figures are svelte and slender-waisted giving the impression of a well-shaped body sharply contoured.

Towards the last years of the Malla supremacy, stone sculpture became stocky and short, as shown by **Vajaramahakala** (page 219). This inscribed sculpture at Svaambhunath is dated 1660 AD and was dedicated by one Jayasimha. Pieces such as these have hardly any resemblance to the exquisite balanced compositions of the past centuries. Medieval art had outlived its youth and declined rapidly. As we have seen, the philosophy by which both Hindu and Buddhist works of art could not be conceived without Tantric connotations was now taken for granted. Their stylistic elements were derived from the examples created in such centres of Tantric learning as Odantapuri, Vikramashila, Nalanda, Sarnath and Jaggaddala; a large number of images, both in stone and bronze, excavated at Sarnath, Nalanda, and Kurkihr are a confirmation of this tradition. The *Patavidhana* part of the *Manjushri-mulakalpa* not only had instructions on the drawing of pictures of the Buddhas, Bodhisattvas and various other gods of the Buddhist pantheon, but also formulae for depicting Shaivite deities such as Shiva, Uma, Karttikeya, etc. This stylistic intermingling of images and the actual interchange of gods between the two religions became an essential feature of Nepalese art from the 14th Century to the present time.

Like the Vyuha forms in Kashmir, several interpretations of Vishnu were also current in Nepal in which the god is depicted with several heads of animals, crowned by the head of a horse. The legend has it that Vishnu had assumed the form of a horse-head deity to kill the demon

VAJRAMAHAKALA, SVAYAMBHUNATH TEMPLE, NEPAL. 1660 AD.

Hayagriva. **A manifestation of Vishnu** (page 213) is an interesting configuration in which Vishnu is shown with the four heads of Garuda (the eagle), a lion, a boar and a demon, over which is the horse's head. His ten hands hold the symbols of Mahadevi which are depicted in several paintings of the Taleju Bhavani temple courtyard. Iconographically, this conception with its many heads and arms is even more fantastic as seen in **Mahishasambara** (page 215). This image which derives from the Bhairavi cult is also owned by the Buddhists who call the deity Yamantaka, the ferocious emanation of Manjushri. In the *Shrimahavajra Bhairava Tantra*, this deity is assigned 16 feet, 34 arms and nine heads, of which the principal head is that of a bull, and the topmost head is that of Manjushri with "irritated expression". He is depicted naked and black in colour, holding all the Tantra symbols, as he steps to one side on one of his legs.

The finest and most popular symbol of the religious, iconographical and stylistic unity of Hinduism and Buddhism is the image of **Ganesha** (page 216). Lord of the Ganas, or Shiva's troops of minor deities, Ganesha is the son of Shiva and Parvati. As remover of obstacles, he is worshipped at the beginning of important undertakings and is especially invoked to gain knowledge, because it was he who wrote down the *Mahabharata* from the dictation by Vyasa. This lovely terracotta sculpture, therefore shews him with a pen in one of his four hands. There are several legends accounting for his elephant head. In Nepal the most popular explanation is that it was a punishment for Shiva who had slain Aditya, the sun. For this violence Kashyapa doomed Shiva's son to lose his head. He, however, restored Ganesha to life again by replacing his human head with that of an elephant, because Shiva had also restored Aditya again to life. Ganesha's elephant head has one tusk because the other was cut off by Parashurama, as Ganesha would not let him into Shiva's presence when this devotee came all the way to Kailasha to pay his respects to the lord of the mountain.

A stylistic analogy with the Ganesha terracotta is the wooden figure, **Yamakinkara** (page 212). Though carved in a different medium and intended to convey a radically different atmosphere, this attendant of Yama, the god of death, still retains a friendly expression on his face and a marvelous feeling of warm flesh. The apparent heaviness is intended, note. The composition is well balanced and agreeable. Yamakinkara is distinguished by the diminutive head of a horse on his crown. The figure wears Sarpakundalas (snake-shaped ear ornaments) and a Nagabhushana (snake ornament around his body) and carries a Pasa (noose) in his left hand; his hand is upheld in a gesture.

The arts of terracotta and wood work are among the most notable artistic achievements of Nepal. The name of the Kathmandu valley, which means the valley of wooden temples, is suggestive of its wooden architecture lavishly decorated with thousands of Tunals (carved brackets). Unfortunately, there is no extant wooden structure that has been

dated earlier than 1394 AD. In the field of terracotta, however, though archaeological evidence is still meagre, it is now certain that examples have survived from as early as the 3rd Century BC. The latest excavations undertaken by the Government Archaeological Department at Dhum Varahi (Chandol) on the outskirts of Kathmandu have revealed a wide variety of curved, hand-pressed moulds intended to cast plaques, for being impressed on to pottery. Animal forms of horses, elephants, lions, cows and buffalos, as well as dancing human figures, are incised in these moulds. On the basis of later Lichhavi inscriptions, these discoveries have been assigned to the 7th-8th Centuries AD. It is very likely that with new excavations a fresh chapter will be added to the already very rich history of the plastic art of Nepal.

The religious art of Nepal is even today a living reality. A class of people called Chitarakaras, professional artists of religious art, flourish and with their phenomenal memories they can reproduce in a few minutes the iconographical details of a host of religious figures.

MADHAVA, KATHMANDU, NEPAL.
13th CENTURY AD.

SIKKIM

Like most Himalayan communities, the people of Sikkim have their all-powerful mountain god, which is regarded by them as a symbol of their safety and prosperity. This is the mountain Kanchenjunga, whose 8,578 meter peak in western Sikkim can be seen on a clear day from almost all parts of the tiny state. The groaning and cracking sound of descending glaciers and of great avalanches tumbling from Kanchenjunga's steep shoulder are a constant source of danger to the Sikkimese, creating a paradoxical attitude in which they identify security with ever-present danger, prosperity with forebodings of disaster. The faith centred on this mountain-god is also derived from the tradition of ancestor-worship. The spirits of ancestors are identified with the fearsome and oblivious Tenmas goddesses, taken over by the Buddhists from Bon beliefs, who live in dark gorges and are sometimes represented by the mountain itself where they dwell.

Against the background of the dazzling beauty of Kanchenjunga, towering over luxuriant pine-covered forests and carpet-like rice fields in terraces precariously spread over the slopes of the deep river valleys, the country presents an incredibly impressive spectacle. Sikkim, a bowl-like basin barely 60 kilometers wide, is enclosed by two steep transverse ridges in the north-south direction, each about 120 kilometers long. In the west, the Singalila crest descending from Kanchenjunga and other giants like Kabru (7,316 meters) and Jano (7,710 meters) marks the boundary with Nepal; and towards the east, the heights of the Donkhya range run along Tibet's frontiers. This range has among its several passes the well-known Nathu-la and Jeleb-la (4,270 meters), which in the past provided trade routes between Sikkim and Tibet through the Chumbi valley.

In the northern region also, Sikkim's boundaries lie with those of Tibet and are roughly demarcated by Himadri, or the Great Himalayan chain. Through this range, among others, are four important passes, namely, Sese-la or Dachi-la (5,286 meters) Kongra-la (5,132 meters), Naku-la (5,269 meters) and Chhorten Nyma-la (5,791 meters). In this region among perpetual glaciers and snow-covered peaks at heights of about 5,486 meters rise several streams which flow through crystalline rocks to form bigger streams called Chhu. Two main streams, the Lachen Chhun in the west and Lachung Chhu towards the east (named after two important monasteries), eventually join together at Chunthang to become Sikkim's principal river, the Tista. This river, flowing south-wards, then cuts across the entire Sikkim basin and, carving out very deep and precipitous gorges, joins near Kalimpong another important river, the Rangit, descending from western Sikkim. Together the two rivers then descend into the Indian plains.

In a small area of 7,300 square kilometers, Sikkim's extensive expanses of trees and foliage are said to contain examples of every type of flora to be found from the Poles to the Tropics. In the south, the bottoms of the valleys, which are sometimes less than 300 meters above

AVALOKITESHVARA PADMAPANI, TASHI DHING MONASTERY, SIKKIM.
18th CENTURY AD.

sea-level, are covered with savannah grassland, while a few kilometers upstream tropical fruits and flowers grow in abundance. The slopes of the outer ranges in the south are covered with a marvellous variety of trees and flowers which according to the seasons display an ever changing scene of colours—green, orange, yellow and crimson, with breath-taking splashes of white as magnolias sway with the wind. The kaleidoscope changes continuously as myriads of brightly coloured butterflies and moths in hundreds of varieties fly among the clusters of foliage.

Sikkim derived its name from the word Sukhim (peace and happiness) and the Tibetans refer to it by the name Denjong (the hidden valley

A DAKINI, NAMCHI MONASTERY, SIKKIM. 17th CENTURY AD.

of rice). It is, therefore, no wonder that this area attracted migrants of a wide range of racial stocks from neighbouring regions. The earliest known settlers in Sikkim were Lepchas from the Assam hills who are said to have come in the 13th Century along with other tribes such as Tamangs and Rais. Tradition also has it that the Lepchas subscribed to the Tantric version of Buddhist beliefs as practised in eastern India. This is very likely because we know from the Tibetan historian Taranatha's description that during this period "the whole of the land of Magadha was conquered and many monks were slain at Odantapuri. This monastery and Vikramashila were destroyed. The Kashmiri pandit

A SIDDHA, NAMCHI MONASTERY, SIKKIM. 17th CENTURY AD.

Shakyashri made his way to Jagardala in Odivisha in the east and having stayed there three years he went on to Tibet. But Ratnarakshita [another renowned pandit who was master of Mantras at Vikramashila] came to Nepal". To avoid the hostile atmosphere in Bengal and Bihar, the comparatively safe route which Shakyashri travelled to Lhasa was possibly through the Chumbi valley either by way of Sikkim or the routes through Bhutan. These tracks were probably also used by other refugees, such as the Lepchas, coming to settle in these areas.

The Buddhists in Sikkim generally belong to the "Red Hat" sect, so called because of the colour of the headgear worn on their ceremonial

233

PADMASAMBHAVA, NAMCHI MONASTERY, SIKKIM. 17th CENTURY AD.

occasions. The "Red Hats" represent the older schools including the Nyingma-pa (ancient) and the Kargyu-pa. The Nyingma-pas trace their origin to the knowledge bequeathed by the Indian saint Padmasambhava (Guru Rinpoche) and favour practices of Yoga involving magical and supra-natural rites. The Kargyu-pas, on the other hand, trace their origin to the teachings of Marpa (1012—97 AD), the master of Mila-repa (1040—1123 AD), based on the Hathayoga schools of the Indian Siddhas. Through psycho-physical exercises such as breath-control and the rapt state of ecstasy, Kargyu-pas seek to achieve objectives similar to those

PANCHAKULA TATHAGATAMANDALA,
SINON MONASTERY, SIKKIM.
EARLY 18th CENTURY AD.

ARHAT NAGASENA,
SINON MONASTERY SIKKIM.
17th—18th CENTURY AD.

that Nyingma-pas also attempt but mainly through scriptures and Mantras. The "Red Hats" are divided into further sub-groups such as the Karma-pas, founded by Tusum Khyen-pa (1110—93 AD); the Drigung-pas, whose leader was Drigung Rinpoche (1143—1216 AD); the Shang-pas, formulated by Shang-Rinpoche (1123—93 AD) and so on. In Sikkim, apart from the Kargyu monasteries of Rumtek, Phodang and Raland, most of the shrines are attributed to the Nyingma-pas. All these sects believed in the conventional set of 84 great Siddhas which were regarded with equal reverence also by the followers of Shiva. This tradition has continued undisturbed to the present day despite the fact that about 60 per cent of the total population of about 170,000 Sikkimese are people of Indo-Aryan stock and profess the Hindu religion.

The earliest known art forms in Sikkim do not go back before the 15th—16th Century AD. These are rather crude carvings in relief placed

A WOODEN MASK, PEMIANGTSE MONASTERY, SIKKIM. 17th CENTURY AD.

on Chhortens (receptacles of worship). A Chhorten is a kind of miniature Stupa, whose original function, that of housing relics of the Buddha or other great teachers, was later combined with ritual significance. Chhortens also marked the route of pilgrims bound for the holy places of Buddhist legend. More than a thousand years after Ashoka built the first Stupas, this architectural design reached Tibet in its maturity in the 8th Century AD. At this time the first recorded Chhortens were built in Tibet at the Samye monastery. The first Chhortens in Sikkim were built after Tibetan models and their shapes were fixed by definite measurements and design. These bulbous structures known as "pots" are built on square-shaped platforms, the "thrones". From the top of the "pots" rise wheels culminating in images of the crescent moon and the sun. Among the relics of various kinds deposited in the hollows of the edifices are Tsha-tsha, or clay figurines representing images of deities, replicas of Chhortens and sometimes sacred inscription. These casts are made of clay kneaded with water and stamped with copper or bronze moulds. In Sikkim there are a number of such Chhortens whose age has not been accurately determined. The earliest stone reliefs used for outer decoration of Chhortens seem to be at Tashi Dhing, going back to a period perhaps before Phuntsog Namgyal (born 1604 AD) who was the first consecrated ruler of Sikkim.

The ascendancy of the Namgyal house marks the beginning of a flowering of Sikkimese art, the cultural influences of which can be traced to the origins claimed by the rulers of Sikkim. The Namgyals claim to be the descendents of the legendary Indian king Indrabodhi who, according to one tradition, was the king of Zahor, or what is now Mandi in Himachal Pradesh. Tibetan tradition considers Indrabodhi to be the spiritual father of Padmasanbhava and places him in the 7th-8th Century AD. He is one of Vajrayana's most eminent personalities and therefore takes his place among the 84 Siddhas. Indrabodhi is linked with the elaboration of the *Guhyasamaja*, a fact which is recorded by Buston (1290—1364 AD) as follows: "Bodhisattva Vajrapani collected in Uddiyana endless revelations of the Vajrayana, made by the Buddha, and gave them to Indrabodhi. Then the land of Uddiyana was emptied and became a large lake full of nagas (serpents). Then Chhaknardorji wrote down the Tantras and after having converted those nagas, he gave the Tantras into their custody. In course of time, the nagas assumed a human form and on the shores of the lake they built a beautiful city, and preaching Vajrayana they obtained great realisation".

By Indrabodhi's time, Mahayana Buddhism had already gone a long way since it first conceived of the idea of Bodhisattvas. The Bodhisattva Avalokiteshvara had been established by the early centuries of the Christian era. In the middle of the 4th Century AD the Yogacharya school was grafted on to the Mahayana doctrine. As recorded by the *Karandavyuha*, belief in the power of Mantras (recitation of formulae) was strengthened by spells for protection against Yakshas, Gandharvas and evil spirits. This cult received great encouragement during the 7th-8th Century AD when the work of casting spells was entrusted to priests called Vidyadharas or the Siddhas. This esoteric doctrine taught that the six-fold bodily and mental happiness could be achieved by Tantras (mystic formulae), Dharanis (litanies) or Mantras (spells), the reciting of which was to be accompanied by music and Mudras (hand gestures). In this way, it was believed, could be obtained supernatural miracle-working powers with the help of Mandalas (magical diagrams). At the same time, the concept of female deities (Taras) was propounded in the *Manjushrimulakalpa*, so that at the root of the Vajrayana pantheon was always Prajna (gnosis) which when symbolised became a goddess, a divine mother or a divine power.

The claim to inheritance of this exciting period of Vajrayana development has most significant implications because it was paralleled, as we have already seen elsewhere, by the equally fascinating progress of its art forms. The Gupta civilisation, though hurt by Ephthalite attacks, subsequently recovered in the shape of "later Gupta" art forms, and eventually merged into medieval Indian culture. Nourished successively by Yashodharman, the Maukharis and the Pushyabhutis, and patronised by powerful emperors, first by the great Harshavardhana of Thanesar and later by the famous Lalitaditya of the Karkota empire in Kashmir, these styles then fanned out, reigning supreme in all those areas which were once controlled by the Kushans. At the basis of these advancing styles were also the refined art forms of the Gurjara-Pratiharas of central India and the Pala art forms from eastern India which then interacted, along the silk road, with Chinese and Iranian art forms and also those of the Uighurs, a Turkish people. Another important branch of Buddhist art with strong Kashmiri influences moved eastwards by the "grand route" and it was this which, via Tibet, finally arrived in Sikkim, carried by the Namgyal dynasty in the early 17th Century.

Until these art prototypes arrived in Tibet it was possible more or less to categorise works of art into different stylistic traditions. Their manners and styles could be distinguished and, as we have seen, related to the interplay of historical and social developments. But already in Tibet it was no longer possible to speak of "schools". At best they could be called "groups", on the evidence of shared characteristics without a chronological or a geographical basis. This metamorphosis in art styles was carried to its logical conclusion in Sikkim, so that it is not possible to refer to even these "groupings" of stylistic influences. The reason for this is not only the late period but also the limited geographical area.

Khye-Bumse, the founder of the Namgyal house, had settled at Phari in the Chumbi valley where he consolidated his position not only through his relationship with the Sakya hierarch (whose daughter he married) but also on account of his deep friendship with the Lepcha chief at Khabe Longtsok. His successors, Mipon Rab, Guru Tashi, Jowo

YAMA, LACHUNG MONASTERY, SIKKIM. 18th—19th CENTURY AD.

THE OFFERINGS, LACHEN MONASTERY, NORTHERN SIKKIM. 18th—19th CENTURY AD.

Nagpo, Jowo Apha and Guru Tenzing, carried forward this tradition and further strengthened their position by taking advantage of the power-vacuum created at that time by the preoccupations of the warring Tibetan factions. For more than a century, there was an uninterrupted and complicated struggle in Tibet between various groups polarized into two main parties. The Phagmotru-pas in central Tibet were opposed by the lords of Samdruptse in Tsang until this bitter struggle was finally brought under control by one of Tibet's greatest figures, Lopsang Gyatso, the Fifth Dalai Lama (1617—82 AD). Towards the south, in the Indian mainland, conditions were also far from settled in the 16th Century AD. After Nilambar of the Khens who ruled over Kamata was overthrown by Alauddin Husain Shah in about 1498 AD, there followed a period of confusion until Biswa Simha of the Koch tribe established a powerful kingdom in 1515 AD with Cooch-Bihar as his capital. But in 1581 AD the kingdom was divided and the feuds between the rulers of the smaller kingdoms led to the intervention of the Ahoms and Muslims, resulting in 1639 AD in the latters' supremacy.

Against this background, Guru Tashi had already moved his capital from Phari to Gangtok and, for reasons of security, the capital was shifted again to Yaksam in western Sikkim by Phuntsog Namgyal early in the 17th Century AD. Phuntsog Namgyal was consecrated as the chief by the famous three lamas in 1642 AD. These lamas were also responsible for laying the foundation of several important monasteries in western Sikkim, such as Pemiangtse and Sinon.

The capital was again moved, this time to Rabdentse, during the reign of Tensung Namgyal (born 1644 AD), who was consecrated in 1670 AD. Genealogical records speak of the quarrels between his three wives and their respective offspring which "laid open Sikkim to foreign invasions". About this time was built the monastery of Namchi. This small but neat and beautiful shrine has, according to the present ruler, the oldest surviving paintings and clay sculptures in Sikkim. **Padmasambhava** (page 234) is a fine clay sculpture, simple and effective. In his deified form, Padmasambhava is represented seated on a lotus with his legs locked. His special symbol is the Khatvanga which he holds in his left arm pressed against his breast. It is said that it was with the Khatvanga that this Indian master had subdued all the malignant gods in Tibet, while he taught the Tantrayogacharya doctrine. With his right hand he holds the Vajra or thunderbolt which was also used in casting spells and exorcizing evil. Padmasambhava is invariably depicted with the Patra or begging bowl in his lap. In the Himalaya his cap is made in a shape which resembles a lotus flower, for, according to tradition, he was born of a lotus.

The interior walls of the Namchi shrine are covered with figures, some beautifully drawn in subdued colours, representing Tantric Buddhist personalities. **A Siddha** (page 233), with Padmasambhava's symbols, is a good example of the painter's complete control over line and colour.

The juxtaposition of shapes and the matching colours are well coordinated, creating a harmonious composition. It is built on a structure of simple outlines, few ornaments and basic forms and, despite the solitary flowing scarf indicating Tibeto-Chinese influence, the overall emphasis is on the pure and essential.

The Siddhas were the Tantrics who were the advocates of psychic culture for attaining Siddhis (supernatural powers). The process of mental and physical exercises through which they gained such Siddhis is called Sadhana. The *Yogasutra*, which is said to be the earliest Sanskrit treatise on the subject, enumerates eight Siddhis, but later works such as the *Brahmavaivarte Purana* mention 34 kinds of Siddhi. In the performance of psycho-physical rites, the presence was essential of a class of females called Dakinis. As bestowers of magical exorcisms and as messengers of divine offerings, they are said to originate in Uddiyana, the country of Padmasambhava in the west, and from there are supposed to have spread towards the east. Dakinis are believed to have given sacred books to Padmasambhava, on which he later founded the doctrine he carried to Tibet from India. They are generally depicted in a gruesome form, but in Tibetan mythology are represented in a more gentle aspect. **A Dakini** (page 232), seen here with a third eye, her peculiarity, and Tantra ornaments, stands naked in a dancing attitude. Dakinis had acquired a new status in the Vajrayana pantheon when they became a part of a new Tantric trilogy, Lama-Yidam-Kandroma, meaning spiritual perception, tutelary divinity and mystic partner. This formula was made after the orthodox Buddhist trilogy, the Buddha-doctrine-congregation.

After Tensung Namgyal, his second wife's son Chador Namgyal (born 1686 AD) became the next ruler, succeeding his father in 1700 AD. It was during Chador Namgyal's rule that important monasteries were built or restored. The Pemiangtse monastery, founded during the reign of the first consecrated ruler, was rebuilt some distance east of the old site. This was done under the supervision of the chief lama, Jigmi Pao, who also built the monastery of Tashi Dhing in 1715 AD.

Avalokiteshvara-Padmapani (page 231) is one of three fine clay statues in the upper chambers of the main shrine at Tashi Dhing. Here Avalokiteshvara-Padmapani is seen in human form but with four arms, two of which are in a "prayer" gesture, while in the other two he holds a lotus and a rosary (fallen off). In the Himalaya, Avalokiteshvara-Padmapani's images usually wear the five-leaf crown, and the divinity is placed in the highest spots in the monastery, representing hill tops, as he is called "the lord that looks down from on high". This also perhaps accounts for his identity with the cult of worshipping mountains, such as Potala which is mentioned in the *Avatamsakasutra*. There are three mount Potalas, of which the one at the mouth of the Indus is legendary. In the 7th Century AD, Hsuan Tsang also mentions Avalokiteshvara who, according to him, manifested himself on mount

Potala in south India. As a lord of mountains, Avalokiteshvara is sometimes represented with five heads, in which case he resembles Shivaas Pancha-anana (see Introduction, page 10).

An interesting clay structure representing **A form of Hevajra** (page 237) is at Pemiangtse, the holy shrine where the present ruler of Sikkim once served as a lama student. This deity, a most popular Tantric figure, is merely the form of Heruka when he is depicted with his Shakti. The symbols and colours of Hevajra are transformed according to the Dhyani buddha family he represents in a particular Sadhana.

This was a natural evolution of the *Guhyasamaja* Tantra (tantra of secret communion), which was the first to reveal the existence of the Tathagata Mandala or the magical circle of five Dhyani buddhas, the progenitors of the five Kullas or families of Buddhist gods and goddesses. The *Sadhanamala* defines the colours of the Dhyani buddhas, Vairocana, Ratnasambhava, Amitabha, Amoghasiddhi and Akshobhaya, as respectively white, yellow, red, green and blue. With the later development of iconometry Shaktis or the female partners in Yab-Yum attitudes also began to be depicted with the five Dhyani buddhas, as shown in **Panchakula Tathagatamandala** (page 235). This symbolises the union of the spiritual and the material corresponding with the Vajradhatu and Garbhadhatu or the "Mandala of the Two Parts". Vajradhatu represents the spiritual aspect, Garbhadhatu the material world. These two aspects are symbolised in this painting representing the divinities and their Shaktis (female energies) in the attitude called Yab-Yum. The Yab is the Dhyani buddha representing the Vajradhatu and the Yum is the respective Shakti symbolising the Garbhadhatu. In the centre is Vairocana, who is the sun, around which revolve in circular motion his manifestations the four other Dhyani buddhas, as planets. Amitabha is on the top of the circle, Amoghasiddhi and Ratnasambhava are on the left and right of Vairocana respectively and Akshobhaya is below. Each Dhyani buddha has his Shakti beside him. Thus Vairocana symbolises "one truth surrounded by four constituent elements".

This painting is in one of the finest surviving monasteries, at Sinon in western Sikkim. It is said to have been built under the patronage of Pedi Wangmo who was Chador Namgyal's half sister, and born of Tensung Namgyal's Bhutanese wife. Her portrait, **Pedi Wangmo** (page 244), in the main chapel of the shrine, is perhaps the finest example of the Sikkimese art of secular portraiture. A remarkable sense of matching colour, a perfect balance of composition and the marvellously intense yet absent-minded expression on her face are created with great success. Her natural poise, as she sits in the attitude called "royal ease" with the right knee lifted and the right arm leisurely draped over it, the unconscious positioning of her delicately shaped hands and her slightly tilted head, are all in complete harmony. The artist has created an exquisite unity of conception and interpretation by placing the

PEDI WANGMO, SINON MONASTERY, SIKKIM.
END OF 17th CENTURY OR EARLY 18th CENTURY AD.

245

figure in between the two symmetrical bands outlining cushions in the background and the two delicately-placed stylised trestles. These motifs do not in the least divert the attention of the viewer from the donor's personality, nor do the background colours disturb the essential simplicity of composition which was so rare during that time.

Thus, Sikkim's greatest contribution to art seems to be in spheres where the artists' imaginations were not restricted by strict, ready-made clichés. In this case, the inner urge and individuality of the painter, no longer supressed by formalism, has obviously broken through the taboos of monastic instructions to portray in relative freedom the subject as he saw and felt. A keen observation of the princess, a shrewd study of her facial expression, her inner personality and her royal dignity are elements that have contributed to produce this beautiful masterpiece.

Pedi Wangmo had opposed the succession of the minor, Chador Namgyal, who fled to Tibet and sought refuge with the Sixth Dalai Lama, while the Rabdentse palace was occupied by the Bhutanese forces. The Bhutanese contingent eventually withdrew and Chador Namgyal returned to Sikkim. But his short-lived rule abruptly came to an end when he became a victim of Pedi Wangmo's conspiracy. In a bizarre scheme reminiscent of the European medieval period, Pedi Wangmo is said to have plotted with a Tibetan doctor, and to have caused the ruler's death by blood letting from his veins. A police force sent by lama Jigmi Pao arrested the doctor and executed him at Namchi along with Pedi Wangmo, who was strangled to death with a silk scarf.

In the chapel at Sinon, masterly use of a few lines and basic colours is observed in the painting **Arhat Nagasena** (page 235). The painters have effectively used the plain, darker colours of the Prabhavali in the background to bring out the standing figure of the saint. The limited spectrum of sober colours with which the face and garments are painted thus stand out, giving an illusion of relief as though the Arhat is about to walk out of the wall. The peaceful face and delicately drawn hands have the same quality as seen in the Pedi Wangmo portrait. In the drawing of this figure, the painters have clearly gone by Indian models even though the facial features are Mongoloid. It is also interesting that this figure was made before the famous Tibetan blocks depicting the sixteen Arhats which, according to manuscripts, were cast by order of Pholhane and his sons (1728-47 AD).

An Arhat is a person who, having mastered the Buddha's teachings, then goes out to impart perfection to others. According to Vajrayana, Gautama Buddha instructed sixteen Arhats to preserve and propagate Buddhism after him. Gautama himself, it is stated, was in one of his incarnations the Arhat Sumedha. It is believed that these Arhats, who may number either five hundred or a group of sixteen (eighteen in China), move collectively from place to place to bless all living beings. They are especially invoked during the laying of temple founda-

THE BUDDHA.   THE BUDDHA WITH A FLOWER OVER EACH EAR.

tions or consecration of objects of worship. Almost every Buddhist
shrine in the Himalaya has paintings or sculptures depicting the Arhats.
The chapel itself in which Pedi Wangmo's portrait and Arhat Nagasena
are painted is made with equally good taste. **The Interior of the Sinon
Shrine** (pages 248-9) shows the altar which according to the general
practice is against the north wall. Among the colourful clay figures of
the divinities, the Buddha is seen sitting in the centre with his right
hand in the Bhumisparsa Mudra (earth touching gesture) while his left
hand is resting on his lap. This gesture is associated with the Great Eng-
lightenment and later was adopted for the images of the Dhyani buddhas, Akshobhaya and Amitabha. According to the usual practice, the
central figure of the Buddha is flanked by two Arhats, namely, Shariputra
on the Buddha's left and Maudgalyayana on his right. The two Arhats are
then flanked by a group of eight Dhyani bodhisattvas in their appropriate

THE INTERIOR OF THE SINON SHRINE, SIKKIM.

family colours. These are Avalokiteshvara, Akshagarbha, Vajrapani, Kshitigarbha, Sarva-nivarana-vishkambhin, Maitreya, Samantabhadra and Manjushri. In front of the divinities is placed the altar on which are the usual ritual objects—the fish motif is of Chinese origin but all the rest are traditional symbols from Indian good-luck omens. The eight auspicious emblems are the white parasol, which wards off "heat of evil desires"; the two gilded fishes, representing "utility and happiness"; the sacred bowl, "the treasury of all desires"; the lotus flower, "pledge of Nirvana or salvation"; the sea-shell, representing "blessedness of turning to the right"; the mystic diagram, "the thread of which leads to bliss"; the standard, "erected on the summit of the shrine"; and the wheel of Dharm, which "leads to perfection". With this group are also other objects with a more specific buddhist symbolism such as the seven jewels and the seven regal symbols. In front of these objects are placed several cups of silver or brass containing the seven offerings of water, flowers, the scented wand, oil, etc. These offerings are symbolic survivals of hospitality in ancient India, given to new arrivals in the monasteries after long and tedious journeys. In addition, there is of course the main vessel with incense which must stay alight day and night.

After a period of regency, Gyurmed Namgyal (born 1707 AD) succeeded his father Chador, in 1717 AD. He inherited a situation which was hardly enviable because there followed a series of raids into Sikkim, first from Nepal and then Bhutan, thus also encouraging internal uprisings with outside help. These disturbed conditions were further aggravated when Gyurmed Namgyal died heirless (1733 AD), just after he gave out that a nun in Sangna Choling was carrying his child. An endless struggle for succession encouraged further Gurkha inroads under Prithvinarayan Shah in the west, matched by several Bhutanese raids by which all land east of the Tista was occupied. These unstable conditions appear to have continued also during the reigns of the sixth ruler, Tenzing Namgyal (born 1769 AD), and his successor, Tsugphud Namgyal (born 1785 AD). The raids and counter-attacks once again forced the Sikkimese to shift their capital which was moved in 1814 to Tumlong during the reign of Tsugphud Namgyal (1793—1864 AD), where it was much better situated and protected by high mountains.

In this atmosphere of turmoil and uncertainty, naturally not much attention could be given to the building of shrines and monasteries. Even those already in existence seem to have been little cared for and rapidly fell into dilapidation. Exceptions are some of the monasteries in the north, such as those at Lachen and Lachung which were protected by the high mountains. These are situated respectively on the western and eastern forklike tributaries that descend from the north to become the river Tista at Chunthang.

Yama (page 240) is a charming wall-painting at Lachung, belonging mostly to folk art even though it is roughly within the confines of liturgical and iconographical precepts. While adhering to traditional methods of drawing, here is an example of the artist obtaining comparative freedom of drawing, here is an example of the artist obtaining comparative freedom of expression, not by pretext of depicting a secular theme, but by his rather naive yet spontaneously untrammelled inspiration. In fact, painters and sculptors of most Himalayan areas from Ladakh to Bhutan during this period impetuously introduced locally-inspired elements which did not conform to ancient rules. Lack of scholarship and, in some cases, outright ignorance sometimes created ingenuous designs which, as in this case, are charming. A notable feature is the manner of drawing the mountain in the shape of a cone which is typically Indian. This is surprising because, although the monastery is close to the famous Tibetan art centres, the painter has rejected the Chinese method of drawing mountains in the shape of "crags in the Dolomites" which had become very popular in Tibet since the Sakya-pa period. The structure of composition, the colours and the simple but effective outlines have here sought to interpret a very popular theme representing the hand-bound Yama being dragged away by Yamantaka, the keeper of hell. Iconographically, Yama is depicted with a bull's head but here the monster has a human head. The skull in the centre which is full of blood is symbolic of Yama's fiery and insatiable thirst for victims whom he devours. According to the legend, when his tyranny became unbearable, the people of the Himalaya appealed to their tutelary deity, Manjushri, who then assumed the fierce form of Yamantaka and defeated and captured Yama.

An equally fascinating painting but with stress more on colour than drawing is **The Offerings** (page 241). This brilliant riot of colours is in the monastery at Lachen. It depicts offerings to the Buddha. The three bags representing three different kinds of grains are placed in front of the altar, while a deer signifies the first sermon of the Buddha which he delivered in the deer park at Varanasi. On the altar are placed three silver plates alternating with three bags of gold and a butter container. On one side of the altar hang traditional silk scarves and on the other, skins of different kinds of animals, fundamental to Ahimsa or non-violence towards humans and animals alike.

BHUTAN

East of Sikki picturesque Bhutan extends to within 250 kilometers of the great bend of the river Brahmaputra. The peaks of Himadri or the Great Himalaya, several of which rise to more than 7,000 meters in northern parts of Bhutan, run across the entire country in an easterly direction but at Kangto (7,090 meters), in the Indian North-East Frontier Agency, these ranges change their direction towards the north-east and terminate at Namcha Barwa (7,756 meters). Forking towards the south from this great northern barrier are gigantic mountain ranges which often take their names from the high passes in their folds. Tule-la, Chilai-la, Pe-la, Dokyong-la, Black mountain, Kula Kangri, Rudong-la and Donga are the ranges from the west to the east. Of these, the Black mountain range between the Punakha and the Tongsa valleys practically divides Bhutan into two distinct cultural spheres.

This almost rectangular country, with an area of about 46,620 square kilometers, is separated from Tibet in the north by the great Himalayan peaks and the "marginal" mountains of the Tibetan plateau. The Tule-la range in the west forms the boundary with Sikkim and in the east the mountain of Tawang marks Bhutan's boundaries with the Indian North-East Frontier Agency area. In the south-east there is a south-westerly range running from a pyramidal mountain 4,130 meters in height to Bhutan's southern borders with India. There are eight principal valleys in Bhutan, of which Paro, Thimphu and Punakha in the middle range of western Bhutan are broad and flat at heights between 1,500 to 2,500 meters and are divided by mountain ranges reaching heights of 3,500 to 4,500 meters. The valleys of the middle region of eastern Bhutan are, on the other hand, comparatively narrow and are sometimes as low as 1,000 meters. With the exception of the rivers Toorsha and Manas which rise in Tibet, the main rivers of Bhutan, such as the Raidak, Sankosh, Tongsa and their tributaries, flow from the southern face of the Himalaya and, winding through defiles at the foot of the mountains, cut through the narrow gorges of the Duars (doors or passes) into the Indian plains and eventually drain into the great river Brahmaputra.

The Duars cut out by these rivers permit access between Bhutan and India just as the river valleys of the Manas and its tributary the Kuri Mhu formed the road for two of the important trade routes linking eastern Bhutan to Lhasa. In the west Bhutan's exit to Tibet and Sikkim was primarily through the passes of Lingshi-la and Yule-la through the Chumbi valley. In this region rises the river Mo which suddenly descends from the lofty snow-covered peaks of Himadri, past Gasa Dzong, to join the river Pho at Punakha and then to become the Sankosh river. Here, the grand castle-monastery of Punakha (1,575 meters) stands on an imposing site commanding a magnificent view of the dark and deep glens from which the two rivers emerge against a backdrop of hills clothed with a variety of trees such as beech, ash, maple, birch, cypress, etc. (pages 20-21). Downstream on the river Sankosh in the Punakha valley are also the beautiful small shrine of

HIMALAYAN ANIMALS.

Bajo and the famous Dzong of Wangdu Phodrang. Further west and almost parallel to the river Sankosh is the river Raidak which flows past Thimphu, the capital of Bhutan, meets its tributary coming through the Paro valley in shape of a fork and eventually cuts through the Duars and emerges into the Indian plains.

Tradition has it that the earliest settlers in the Bhutan valleys were nomadic tribes from eastern India, particularly Cooch-Bihar. Due to inadequate research into their mode of living, customs and traditional arts, Bhutan's known cultural heritage does not go back earlier than the late 15th Century. It was then that several lamas living in neighbouring regions of Tibet are said to have crossed the Wagay pass into Bhutan to escape the holocausts among the quarrelling power groups in Tibet. As already referred to in the chapter on Sikkim, this was a period of Tibetan history when for almost a century it is difficult to follow the course of events because of civil war. Lhasa's authority had diminished and seats of power had shifted to Tsetang and Neudong on the one hand, and Rinpung and Samdruptse on the other. To escape this mounting struggle between opposing clans, several lamas appear to have come down from Rinpung and surrounding areas to Gasa, which according to tradition is among Bhutan's earliest monasteries. The fanciful legend tells how a Guru or master entered Bhutan with a goat, a bag of rice and a yakload of salt. The skeleton of a goat and a saddle, still preserved at the Gasa Dzong, are said to have belonged to him. The discovery, as it were, of a heavenly country with forest-clad mountains stretching in every direction, magnificent waterfalls and mountain rapids and, more than anything, abundance of food grains, brought from Tibet several group of Kham adventurers who were asociated with the Rindpung-pas. These were essentially nomadic people who lived in tents and where called Garpa ("those of the camp"). Also, in contrast to their adversaires the Phagmotru-pas who owed allegiance to the "Yellow Hat" sect of Vajrayana Buddhism, these newcomers in Bhutan, like their allies, belonged to the "Red Hat" sect.

The Tephoo Bhutias, according to tradition, the original inhabitants of Bhutan, readily accepted the way of life of the "Red Hat" sect, as these people were already well disposed towards similar Tantric Hindu and Buddhist cults in eastern India. But they also thus inherited the politico-religious rivalries of Tibet where powerful religious communities were locked in a struggle to the finish. Bhutan now found itself in the camp of the "Red Hats"—the Karma-pa or the Kargyu-pa sects, and their allies, the Nyingma-pas (the ancients)—against the "Yellow Hats", also called the Geluk-pa, a sect which was founded by Tsongkha-pa (1357—1419 AD).

The rise to power in Tibet of the Fifth Dalai Lama (1617—82 AD) who had called for help from the Mongol king, Gushri Khan, in the putting down of his adversaries, the Karma-pas and the Tsang, boded ill for Bhutan, the allies of the latter. The king of Tsang was killed in battle in 1642 AD and, hard-pressed by Gushri Khan, the Garpa general who was active in the Lho Brag region escaped to southern Tibet, where he could rely on help from Bhutan, ruled at this time by Kargyu-pa priest-kings. Anticipating attack by the "Yellow Hat" forces, Bhutan's old capital Punakha feverishly strengthened her defences. The already formidable castle-monastery at Punakha, which was founded in 1527 AD, became a great fort. Thus also rose the great fortress-monasteries of Wangdu Phodrang, Simtokha and Thimphu, situated as they were in strategic places either surrounded by the waters of rivers or on top of hills commanding a good all-round view. Bhutan's fears were realised when Punakha was attacked in 1648 AD by an expedition sent from Bus. The attack, however, failed partly because of the inefficiency (or

VAJRASATTVA, PUNAKHA SHRINE, BHUTAN. 17th CENTURY AD.

perhaps complicity) of the Fifth Dalai Lama's regent, Norbu, who, in fact, later led a revolt against his master from Shigatse. A few years later, Bhutan retaliated. Its raids into Tibet first in 1669 AD and then in 1671 AD were checked, but the atmosphere of continuous hostility between Tibet and Bhutan persisted so that in the following period when practically all Tibet acknowledged the supremacy of "Yellow Hats", the Bhutanese maintained their cultural identity in the orbit of the "Red Hat" faith.

Among the many refugees who crossed into Bhutan at this time seem to have been quite a few craftsmen, as is evident from the numbers of studios and shops for bronze casting established at the Punakha, Simtokha and Thimphu Dzongs. In the Punakha Dzong there are remnants of a foundry for bronze casting which is said to have been started early in the 16th Century AD. This is not surprising as the eastern Tibetan province of Kham from which most refugees came to Bhutan was already famous for its Kham-so (made in Kham) bronzes. There were well-known centres for bronze casting at Degi, Chamdo and Reochi in Kham, where different types of bronzes were made. These included the three kinds of Indian bronzes, namely, Sharli, U-li and Nupli, which originated respectively in eastern, central and western India. The well-known "yellow bronze" called Kadam Lima, which was also in great demand, was introduced in the 11th Century AD by the Indian saint Atisha, then he came to preach Buddhism in Tibet. In Tsang, too, at Tsedong there was an old school of sculptors which was founded in the 10th Century AD by the Sakya lamas. **The Buddha** (page 17) in Bhumisparsa Mudra is an early and rare bronze made in Bhutan. It will be noticed that while the face is moulded in perfect proportion and displays a beautifully serene expression, the hands and feet are rather heavily made and are not in keeping with the elegant figure. This feature is typical of the Bhutanese style in which a number of images of Bon deities also seem to have been made during this period. The Bon-po faith seems to have had a considerable following in Bhutan and even today in the country's interior people subscribe to its Shamanistic practices. Its chief priests, called Shen, exercised great authority and played a prominent part in rituals and funeral ceremonies which required the sacrifice of many victims. Its religious leader was Miwo Shenrap, a native of western Tibet, who appears to have been greatly influenced by popular forms of Shaivism and took over some of its rites as practised in Kashmir and in the Punjab Hills. The iconography of its art forms also absorbed many Tantric symbols associated with Shiva's worship.

Apart from the well-known *cire perdus* method of bronze casting in which the model was made first in beeswax, a very popular technique of casting was through the use of clay models. The clay figure, cut into two halves, was baked in terracotta and from these pieces moulds were made for casting the image in molten bronze. The latter method of

THE BUDDHA WITH VAJRAPANI AND VAIROCANA, SIMTOKHA MONASTERY, BHUTAN.
17th CENTURY AD.

bronze casting appears to have become increasingly popular in Bhutan as the sculptors acquired greater proficiency in the making of clay figures.

The surviving works of art in the Punakha Dzong belong to the 17th Century AD and the later period. A lovely large sculpture in clay in one of the main chapels of Punakha is **The Buddha** (page 274) sitting in the earth-touching attitude on a double-lotus throne. The tradition of commissioning large statues to earn proportionately more merit had already become a popular custom in the Himalaya during the 7th Century AD. This tradition was carried on in Bhutan in the plastic medium of clay instead of stone. Terracotta, of course, was known from time immemorial, but the practice of making gigantic figures in clay perhaps originated in the oasis of Khotang in Central Asia where, in the absence of stone quarries, there was no option but to work in the available plastic medium, namely, clay. These statues were profusely painted and gilded to give an appearance of metal and wrapped in the robes appropriate to the status and significance of the divinities. Ritual required that the gilded patina be renewed annually.

With greater specialisation and as the monasteries became richer, the practice of gilding figures of clay was replaced by that of covering them with thin plates of metal designed in a kind of shell to cover the entire figure except the face. This "shell" was mostly made by beating the metal plates into shape, and some ornamental parts were added to this by casting. One such beautiful example covered with "silver" plate is **Vajrasattva** (page 257). This gigantic and impressive sculpture obviously evoking a divine presence is constructed within the confines of rules laid down by Indian patterns. Its meditative stillness, like its gilded patina, is on the surface and does not impart that indescribable atmosphere of spirituality to be seen in early Buddhist art. Only when it comes to details is it that the talent of the Bhutanese craftsmen appears, in their ingenuity of ornamentation. This decorative sense is beautifully used in making the crown that Vajrasattva wears, and also his robes with their embroideries, emblems, etc.

Vajrasattva's status in the Vajrayana pantheon is anomalous. He is generally regarded as the sixth Dhyani buddha and also as the priest of the other five. His worship is essentially secretive in nature and especially in his Yab-Yum form he is not shown in public. His elaborate crown, rich robes and ornaments distinguish him from the other austerely dressed Dhyani buddhas, as he sits cross-legged but exhibiting no special hand gesture. He carries the Vajra in his right hand with his palm upwards against his chest and the Ghanta (bell) in the left hand which rests in his lap or against his left thigh. His second name is Dharmadhatu.

The walls of the Punakha chapel are lavishly covered with paintings which are mostly late except for a few rooms containing 17th Century AD paintings. These mainly depict either Mandalas or life stories of the Siddhas. The legends of Buddha's life, events which had again become important under Tsongkha-pas influence in most other parts of the Himalaya, are here conspicuously missing. **A Siddha's Life Story** (page 280) probably depicts events in the life of the Siddha Lutsoka, a Brahman from Bengal. The mystic was disillusioned when he saw many people dying. He abandoned the world to take refuge in the solitude of a nearby forest. His meditation, however, was of no avail until he met a Yogi who initiated him in the mysteries of Tantricism. After twelve

HIMALAYAN ANIMALS.

years of meditation and practice of the *Guhyasamaja* Tantra, he comprehended the truth that Nirvana (absolute deliverance) and Samsara (worldly life) do not exist separately. Thus, he obtained salvation.

The technique of applying colours on the walls, and manner of line drawing and composition here are very similar to those in other parts of the Himalaya. They are essentially derived from the Ajanta methods, by which the pictorial composition is built round the central figure. The main, rather large figure, is the focal point towards which flock the adoring smaller divinities, while other divine beings, either singly or part of scenes from traditional stories, cover the outer areas. The central figure is usually motionless in a static ritual pose, but as the scenes spread out, more and more movement is felt, compensating to some extent for the rigidity of the principal divinity. The elements in the outer fringes are interlocked and are spread over the walls in long compositions that gradually unfold as the devotee slowly walks along

261

THE COURT OF CHHOIKYONG, WANGDU PHODRANG MONASTERY, BHUTAN. 17th CENTURY AD.

the wall from left to right. Once the theme is picked up, different scenes can be made out in groups interconnected by subsidiary characters, animals or foliage. The events depicted are not necessarily placed in sequence so that often their interpretation becomes a very arduous task indeed, especially as the life stories of the different Siddhas greatly resemble each other. A redeeming factor in these rather stylised paintings is the use of bright colours and the interplay of broad areas of greens, depicting mountains, clouds and foliage as though reflecting the lovely Bhutanese landscape.

In what are called Goinkhangs, there is another group of wall-paintings which are reserved for the inmates of the demoniac world. A Goinkhang is usually a small dark room in a lonely corner of the monastery, in the gloom of which are hung skins, teeth and nails of animals, and also the remains of sacrificial victims or enemies together with their weapons, armour, etc. These are erected as effigies, dressed in their original clothes, and usually the skulls are covered with masks. **A Bhayankara Effigy** (page 278) is one such example in the Wangdu-Phodrang Goinkhang. In this room are also some extraordinary paintings, such as **The Court of Chhoikyong** (pages 262-63), depicting misshapen forms of demons, black magicians, witches, ferocious animals, vultures, etc. This is one of the groups taken from the "wheel of existence" whose six different sections illustrate the world's unreality to which every living being in this world is inextricably bound. The cycle of births and deaths, caused by human ignorance, is enacted here in all its sorrows and pains until finally it points the path of salvation. It corresponds precisely to the Indian tradition, an ageless wisdom repeatedly revealed, lost and then restored through the cycle of ages. The "wheel of existence" is depicted in the shape of a circle which Mara, the lord of death, holds in his teeth and in between his arms and legs. Round the edge of the circle are twelve small inset pictures representing the twelve-fold causal nexus binding living beings to the sorrows of the inner circle. In the centre of the circle are a cock, a snake and a pig, representing passion, anger and ignorance. The space between the outer rim and central axis is divided into six segments, of which the three top segments representing happier spheres of existence are in complete contrast to the three lower parts about woeful rebirths. Here, the Chhoikyong, or Dharmapala, occupying the centre of the stage is surrounded by evil spirits, animals that kill each other or are slain by men, sinners who are tormented by hunger or thirst or tortured by fires of hell. These characters look terrifying, the animals are ferocious, while the sky is infested with vultures and other equally avaricious birds.

As in the drawing of the divine figures, Indian iconometry also had set rules for Bhayankara (terrifying) figures. The artist, however, had apparently a greater freedom of action here as long as he successfully enlarged and improved upon this grotesque world of frenzied terror. He was permitted to dissolve in his imagination the realities of human

264

AVALOKITESHVARA, SIMTOKHA MONASTERY, BHUTAN. 17th CENTURY AD.

form and then express graphically the horrifying vision which he could conceive on his own. Thus, in some of the dark, eerie corners of these Goinkhangs can be seen examples of paintings for which the credit can largely be claimed by Bhutanese artists.

Despite some brilliant visions created by the artists in the world of Chhoikyong, most of the paintings in Goinkhangs are stylised, lack proportions and are weakened by their exaggeration. Despite the dramatic tension created by the rough nakedness of the characters charged with latent passion, the overall effect is static and unconvincing. The grimacing mask-like faces expressing anger and fear seem to be as lifeless as their miming gestures. The convulsed movements are stylised and, although weird and unfamiliar forms arouse a degree of curiosity, they are devoid of emotional content.

The baffling variety of characters, gesture and symbols depicted here

PUTALOKHI, THIMPHU DZONG MONASTERY, BHUTAN. 18th CENTURY AD.

are paralleled by an equally confusing mixture of styles apparently picked up at random from various sources. The drawings of the various birds and animals clearly follow the Indian style, which was seen for the first time at Ajanta and which became very popular all over Asia through the Sanskrit story-collection called the *Panchatantra*. Since the first centuries after Christ this treatise has been translated into more than fifty languages under different names, for instance the *Kalilah and Dimnah*, an Arabic version of about 750 AD. On the other hand, the central figures including Chhoikyong and his companions display strong Chinese stylistic influence which apparently came via the

266

GARUDA, THIMPHU DZONG MONASTERY, BHUTAN. 16th—17th CENTURY AD.

nearby art centres at Kham. This is particularly noticeable in the head-dresses and gowns worn by the principal figures. With the Indian foundations on which Buddhist art was built and the proximity of Kham where Chinese provincial art was always strong, these two tendencies were inevitable. But a new element seen here is the remarkable affinity which some of the figures in the lowest row have with some of the Mongol paintings depicting the life of the nomads. These drawings resemble a group of Mongol pictures under the signature "Master Mehmed, the black pen" that have been found in recent years depicting terrifying demons and scenes from sacrifice and worship which are evidently Shamanistic. Like the so-called "black pen" paintings, the beasts and demons of Chhoikyong's court also display a strong linear emphasis. The colours are few, namely, blue-black, red and brown, and the crude attempt occasionally made to produce an illusion of roundness by patches of colour has merely served to produce a kind of shadow-play.

267

The analogy is particularly striking in the drawing of rough and crude hands and feet which appear to be prompted by some mysterious nervousness.

This stylistic connection with history can be traced from the time of the old Sakya-parties with the Mongols when the Mongol court showed considerable sympathy to Lamaism. Later, Soinam-Gyatso (the Third Dalai Lama and the abbot of Drepung) obtained an edict from the Mongol king Altan Khan in 1578 AD abolishing animal sacrifices and in return, as it were, Genghis Khan and even some Shamanistic deities were included in the Lamaist pantheon. The Mongols took advantage of this position: after Soinam Gyatso's death, his reincarnation, the Fourth Dalai Lama, Yointen-Gyatso (1589—1617 AD), was none other than a great-grandson of Altan Khan himself. Thus while the Geluk-pas had firmly linked their destiny with the Mongols, the Karma-pas and Tsang were allied to Ligden Khan of the Chahars. Therefore it is understandable that Mongol stylistic influences, especially those portraying Shamanistic themes, should have penetrated the Himalaya. What is intriguing is the actual process of the entry of these influences into Bhutan, particularly after Ligden Khan of the Chahars was killed by Gushri Khan of the Khoshots and Bhutan came into conflict with the "Yellow Hats".

It is interesting to note that the three groups of styles on just this one wall conform to the Tibetan tradition of absorbing different styles from great civilisations in the neighbourhood and yet keeping these mannerisms apart. For instance, in the Tibetan monastery of Samye (built c. 775 AD), which was designed in imitation of the famous Indian monastery of Odantapuri, each of its three storeys has a different style—the palace on the top floor was designed in an Indian manner, the second floor in Chinese fashion and the first floor according to the style imported from Li (Khotan).

The freedom with which the Bhutanese craftsmen discarded the basic conventions in order to reveal the world of fantasy of the Goinkhangs was completely surrendered when it came to the basic divine image of the Buddha. As shown by **The Buddha** (page 271), the painters once again followed India's ancient precepts, laid down mostly in the treatises of the Gupta period. The poise of the body and the expression of serenity and religious ecstasy on the face have the simplicity and sculptural solidity of the classical figures of the Sarnath school. The sheath-like transparent garments, made even more translucent by simple but definite lines, have imbued the icon with a beautiful feeling of aliveness. The artists have thus succeeded in transferring the virtues of the Gupta style to the image despite rather strict repetition of the sacred originals.

Inevitably, in doing so, some of the native traits have also crept in. This is particularly seen in the slightly exaggerated metaphorical character of individual features reflecting local characteristics. This element is well absorbed into the composition. The only discordant

A VIEW OF THE TAK-SANG MONASTERY, BHUTAN.

note, perhaps, is in the drawing of the swelling palms of the hands and similarly rather large and unnatural big toes. These irksome stylisations are, however, toned down by the grace of the svelte, smooth torso and limbs and also the pliant curves of the elongated fingers.

The colour of the divine image, like its structure, was laid down by rite and convention. In the older paintings there is a uniformity in which few colours—such as reds, blues and greens—predominate in soft shades. These pure colours are applied with hardly any shading, so that a figure does not emerge as a result of light and shade, but as a kind of pattern outlined to form shapes. It is as though this is another version of the Mandala (magical diagram), in which the psycho-physical world and divine powers are brought within the limits of circles, squares and triangles.

The method of painting employed in Bhutan is similar to the technique used for all painting elsewhere in the Himalaya. On a moist wall a series of coats of an emulsion of lime and gum were applied, and then polished with a smooth surface such as a conch shell. An outline of the subject according to the rules was then sketched in Indian ink or charcoal and, beginning with the central figure, subsidiary subjects were similarly drawn. Then the various colours in diluted form were applied with a brush in several coats. To strengthen the colour, the painting was covered with a varnish consisting of a mixture of glue, lime and the appropriate colour. The colours used in Bhutan seem to be both organic and inorganic: cochineal for red, lapis-lazuli for blue, arsenic for yellow and a mixture of arsenic with lapis-lazuli in different proportions to produce greens in a variety of shades.

About a hundred years after the first outburst of activity in building fortress-like monasteries in the face of danger of foreign attacks in the 16th Century, there was again a period of renewed activity to make the shrines more resplendent. The chief factor in this progress appears to have been the appointment of four Penlops (governors) at Thaga, Thimphu, Tongsa and Tashigong by Tenzing Dukgyag, the first Deb Raja (temporal ruler). Tenzing Dukgyag although owing allegiance to the Dharma Raja (spiritual ruler) in the person of Lama Shubdung Ngawang Namgyal, thus participated in the dual control of the state by the clergy and the laity. Authority having been divided between the spiritual and the temporal chiefs, as well as the powerful governors of the four regions, a situation developed which was very much like that in the three divided Malla kingdoms in Nepal. Quarrels and divisions followed and the rulers, vying with each other for greater power and glory, also erected religious monuments which each claimed to be better, bigger and more resplendent than the others.

The Simtokha monastery, which was also originally founded about the same time as those of Punakha and Wangdu Phodrang, now greatly benefited from rivalry between the divided regions. Huge statues of clay called Dzaku were made, such as **Avalokiteshvara** (page 265). This

THE SEVEN SACRED JEWELS.

is a gigantic statue whose eleven heads and eight principal arms are conventionally made, as seen in a similar thousand-eyed and thousand-armed Bodhisattva called Chentong Chhaktong (referred to on page 117). What is unusual here is the Prabhavali (gate of honour), whose marvellous elaboration surpasses every other decoration hitherto seen in the Himalaya. The artists who could not disobey the set commands of iconography in the construction of the main figure of the deity to prescribed proportions, seem to have concentrated on these marginal motifs to display their capacity for decoration and skill in handicrafts. With its vast size and the shifting forms and rhythm of the leaves, flowers and twigs, in which even birds are interwoven in a fantastic mass of complicated designs, it is a marvel of patient and painstaking work. The concept as a whole here is very much like the tympanum of the gilded copper doorways seen in 17th Century Nepal. Here, also, the principal object of devotion is placed within an arch formed by the divinity's several hands which is then again surrounded by a large circular decorative border. On the top is the ever-present figure of

THE EIGHT AUSPICIOUS INGREDIENTS.

Garuda, seen here in human form with wings and cymbals held in two hands, as compared with the conventional Nepalese Garudas with hands raised and legs clutching coiled serpents. The stone Kalasha (flower vase) placed over a round, three-tiered pedestal in Nepal is replaced here by the two stylised peacocks on similar stands. The goddesses Shari and Lakshmi on the right and left respectively are replaced by two Taras. In style, too, these two female divinities with their supple limbs and elegant figures greatly resemble their Nepalese counterparts. Among the many legends about the origin of Taras the most popular is that they were born from the tears shed by Avalokiteshvara, and thus represent his never-ceasing grief at the miseries of mankind.

Constructed in a similar style is **Shariputra and Vajrapani** (page 275). This is in the main chapel at Simtokha which has ten such figures of Arhats and Dhyani Bodhisattvas all over two meters high and flanking the main gigantic figure of the Buddha. The earliest Buddhist triad of Buddha-Dharma-Samgha (Budda-the law-the assembly) was represented by the Buddha with Avalokiteshvara and Manjushri, the latter some-

THE BUDDHA. PUNAKHA SHRINE, BHUTAN. 17th CENTURY AD.

times being replaced by Maitreya. Another group consisted of the Buddha accompanied by his two favourite disciples—Shariputra towards the left and Maudgalyayana "the right-hand disciple of Gautama". This triad is surrounded by the eight Bodhisattvas, among whom is Vajrapani.

The Dhyani Bodhisattva Vajrapani has been identified with the Hindu god Indra and later Vishnu. A legend, similar to that associated with Vishnu, states that all the Buddhas met together on the top of mount Meru and decided to get hold of the Amrita (the nectar of immortality), which lay at the bottom of the sea. By churning the ocean with mount Meru they obtained the Amrita from the evil demons and kept it in Vajrapani's custody. The monster Rahu, however, stole the Amrita, so that a fearful struggle followed in which the Amrita was defiled with poison. As a punishment, Vajrapani was forced to drink it, whereupon he became dark-blue in colour.

Vajrapani's blue image is seen in the wall-painting covering a whole wall in the main hall of worship at Simtokha. **The Buddha with Vajrapani and Vairocana** (page 259) shows the Buddha in the Bhumi-sparsa mudra with Vajrapani on his right and Vairocana on his left. Vairocana is depicted with four heads and wears a Bodhisattva crown. With his right hand he displays the Varadha mudra while in his left is his symbol, a wheel. This large, impressive painting is typical of the late period when almost every element was highly stylised and every nook and corner was crammed with figures and symbols.

In Bhutan, sculpture in stone was not as popular as in India. This medium was mostly utilised in carving out bas-reliefs, used for the outer walls of Chhortens and monasteries, and generally depicted portraits of the Siddhas. The Siddhas are the most eminent esoteric personalities of medieval India. They represent an intimate bond between Vajrayana Buddhism and Hindu Shivaism, expressing the same mystical urge through similar ideas and symbols. **Putalokhi** (page 266) is a fine bas-relief in black slate stone at the Thimphu Dzong. This is inscribed with the name "Putalokhi 34". The number probably refers to the position of the Siddha in the hierarchy, even though the name has not been exactly identified with any of the 84 Siddhas. Probably the representation is of Pu-ta-li, which is another name for the Siddha Nagabodhi. According to the legend, when the Siddha was living in the golden temple in western India, a thief approached him with the intention of stealing his golden bowl. The all-knowing master, without waiting for the thief to commit the crime, himself offered him the bowl. Amazed at this gesture, the thief repented and begged for spiritual guidance. Thus, he was eventually freed from all worldly desire.

Like Nepal, Bhutan had an important art school of wood carving, the raw material for which was found in abundant variety in its forests. Tradition has it that sandalwood statues from India were imported and consecrated in important shrines, and, according to one record, craftsmen from Cooch-Bihar were employed in large numbers. A beauti-

SHARIPUTRA AND VAJRAPANI, SIMTOKHA MONASTERY, BHUTAN. 17th CENTURY AD

A JATAKA LEGEND.

ful piece in the Thimphu Dzong is **Garuda** (page 267). The mythical sun-eagle, a most popular divinity of Hinduism, was also owned by Vajrayana Buddhism and associated with Vajrapani. The famous Chinese pilgrim, Hsuan Tsang, mentions that Vajrapani was connected with subduing the gigantic snake in Uddiyana. It is also believed that when the nagas (serpents) came to listen to the Buddha's sermons, it was Vajrapani's duty to protect them from their mortal enemy, the Garuda. To do so, Vajrapani assumed the shape of a Garuda and is thus usually depicted on the top of the Prabhavalis of important Buddhist divinities.

Even though Bhutan's art history had a late start in about the 15th Century AD its artistic heritage is very rich and varied, as seen in the few examples of its treasures reproduced here.

A BHAYANKARA EFFIGY, WANGDU PHODRANG MONASTERY, BHUTAN. 16th—17th CENTURY AD.

A SIDDHA'S LIFE STORY, PUNAKHA MONASTERY, BHUTAN. 17th CENTURY AD.

BIBLIOGRAPHY

Archer, W. G. *Indian Painting in the Punjab Hills*, London, 1952

Bamzai, P. N. K. *A History of Kashmir*, Delhi, 1962

Banerjee, N.R. *Nepalese Art, (An Introduction)*, Kathmandu, 1966

Barrett, Douglas and Gray, Basil *Painting of India*, Geneva, 1963

Bhattacharya, Benoytosh *The Indian Buddhist Iconography*, Calcutta, 1958

Brown, Percy *Tours in Sikkim and Darjeeling District*, Calcutta, 1922

Bussagli, Mario *Painting of Central Asia*, Geneva, 1963

Chandra, Moti *Jain Miniature Paintings from Western India*, Ahmedabad, 1949

Coomaraswamy, A. K. *Rajput Painting*, Oxford, 1916

Dalai Lama, The *An Introduction to Buddhism*, 1960

Davis, Hassoldt *Nepal, Land of Mystery*, London, 1959

Fisher, M. W. and others *Himalayan Battleground*, New York, 1963

Forbes, Duncan *The Heart of Nepal*, London, 1962

Franche, A. H. *A History of Western Tibet*, London

French, J. C. *Himalayan Art*, London, 1931

Ganhar, J. N. and P. N. *Buddhism in Kashmir and Ladakh*, New Delhi, 1956

Getty, Alice *The Gods of Northern Buddhism*, Tokyo, 1962

Goetz, Hermann *The Early Wooden Temples of Chamba*, Leiden, 1955; *India, Five Thousand Years of Indian Art*, London, 1959

Hagen, Tony and others *Nepal*, Berne, 1961

Hedin, Sven *Central Asia and Tibet*, London, 1903; *Trans-Himalaya*, London, 1909-13; *The Silk Road*, London, 1938

Ipsiroglu, M. S. *Painting and Culture of the Mongols*, London, 1967

Karan, Pradyumna and Jenkins, W. M. *The Himalayan Kingdoms, Bhutan, Sikkim and Nepal*, Princeton, 1963

Kazi, Sonam Topgay *Tibet House Second Exhibition Catalogue*, 1966

Khandalawala, Karl *Indian Sculpture and Painting*, Bombay, 1938; *Pahari Miniature Painting*, Bombay, 1958

Khosla, G. D. *Himalayan Circuit*, London, 1965

Kramrisch, Stella *The Art of Nepal*, (The Asia Society Catalogue), New York, 1964

Krishnadasa, Rai *Mughal Miniatures*, New Delhi, 1959

Lamas of Ladakh Monasteries [Compiled by] *History of Ladakh*, 1959

Leifer, Walter *Himalaya, Mountain of Destiny*, London, 1962

Louis, J. A. H. *The Gates of Tibet*, Calcutta, 1894

McLeish, Alexander *The Frontier Peoples of India*, London, 1931

Mason, Kenneth *Routes in the Western Himalaya*, Calcutta, 1929

Mehta, N. C. *Studies in Indian Painting*, Bombay, 1926

Namgyal, Thutol *History of Sikkim*, Calcutta; *Gazetteer of Kashmir and Ladakh*, Calcutta, 1890

Nebesky-Wojkowitz, René Von *Where the Gods are Mountains*, London, 1956

Pallis, Marco *Peaks and Lamas*, London, 1940

Panikkar, K. M. *A survey of Indian History*, Bombay, 1963

Pant, S. D. *The Social Economy of the Himalayans*, London, 1935

Petech, Luciano *A Study of the Chronicles of Ladakh*, Calcutta, 1939; *Mediaeval History of Nepal*, (750—1480 AD), Rome, 1958; *Asia Centrale*, Milan, 1960

Randhawa, M. S. *Kangra Valley Painting*, New Delhi, 1954

Ray, S. C. *Early History and Culture of Kashmir*, Calcutta, 1957

Regmi, D. R. *Ancient Nepal*, Calcutta, 1960; *Medieval Nepal*, Part I and II, Calcutta, 1965-6

Risle, H. H. *Introduction to Gazetteer of Sikkim*, Calcutta, 1894

Roerich, Nicholas *Himalayas, Abode of Light*, Bombay, 1947

Rowland, Benjamin Jr *The Wall-paintings of India, Central Asia and Ceylon*, Boston, 1938; *The Evolution of the Buddha Image*, New York, 1961

Sikkim Government of Pub. *Sikkim, A Concise Chronicle*

Singh, Madanjeet *Indian Sculptures in Bronze and Stone*, Rome, 1952; *India*, UNESCO World Art Series, Paris, 1954; *Ajanta*, London and New York, 1965

Snellgrove, David *Buddhist Himalaya*, Oxford, 1957

Stein, M. A. *Sand Buried Ruins of Khotan*, London, 1903

Thapa, N. B. *A Short History of Nepal*, Nepal

Tucci, Giuseppe *Tibetan Painted Scrolls*, Rome, 1949; *Preliminary Report on two Scientific Expeditions in Nepal*, Rome, 1956; *Tibet, Land of Snows*, London, 1967

White, John Claude *Sikkim and Bhutan*, London, 1909

Wright, Daniel *History of Nepal, Calcutta*, 1958 (Reprint)

Younghusband, Francis *The Heart of a Continent*, London, 1896

Zimmer, Heinrich *Myths and Symbols in India Art and Civilization*, New York, 1946

LIST OF PLATES

283

LIST OF FIGURES

All the figures reproduced here are from a sketch book of the Head Lama Lobzang Tsulthim (1865-1926), of Risong monastery, Ladakh, except the figures on pages 19, 47, 51, 71, 247, 272 and 273, which are printed by courtesy of Tibet House Museum, New Delhi. Figures on pages 165, 179, 187 and 209 are reproduced from walls of a private house in Bhatgaon, Nepal.

286

Filmset in Great Britain by Bookprint Limited, Crawley, Sussex

Printed in Italy by Amilcare Pizzi S.p.A.

UNITED NATIONS EDUCATIONAL, SCIENTIFIC AND CULTURAL ORGANIZATION, PARIS